I0503929

Crafting Connections

The Art of Speech and the Power of Communication

By Khaled bouajaja

Content

Chapter 1: Foundations of Effective Communication

Subchapter 1: Understanding the Importance of Communication

Introduction:

Effective communication is the cornerstone of human interaction. It is a process through which information, ideas, and emotions are exchanged between individuals, enabling us to connect, collaborate, and understand one another. Communication plays a vital role in every aspect of our lives, from personal relationships to professional success. In this subchapter, we will explore the significance of communication, its impact on various areas of life, and the benefits of developing strong communication skills.

The Essence of Communication:

At its core, communication is about conveying meaning and understanding. It involves not only the exchange of words but also nonverbal cues, such as body language, facial expressions, and tone of voice. Effective communication requires active listening, empathy, and the ability to adapt to different situations and audiences. It serves as a tool for self-expression, building relationships, resolving conflicts, and fostering collaboration.

Communication in Personal Relationships:

Strong communication forms the foundation of healthy personal relationships. It enables individuals to express their needs, desires, and emotions, fostering understanding and empathy between partners, family members, and friends. Effective communication helps in resolving conflicts, enhancing intimacy, and nurturing trust. It promotes mutual respect, active engagement, and emotional support, leading to more fulfilling and satisfying relationships.

Communication in the Workplace:

In the professional realm, effective communication is essential for success. Clear and concise communication ensures that tasks are carried out efficiently, objectives are understood, and expectations are met. It facilitates teamwork, collaboration, and innovation within organizations. Good communication skills enable leaders to inspire and motivate their teams, provide constructive feedback, and navigate conflicts. It also plays a crucial role in networking, building professional relationships, and advancing careers.

Communication in Education:

Communication is vital in the field of education, as it is the primary means of imparting knowledge and facilitating learning. Teachers must effectively communicate instructions, explanations, and concepts to students, ensuring understanding and engagement. Students, in turn, need strong communication skills to ask questions, seek clarification, and express their thoughts and ideas. Communication in education extends beyond the classroom, encompassing interactions with parents, administrators, and peers.

Communication in Healthcare:

In healthcare settings, clear and effective communication is crucial for patient care and safety. Healthcare professionals must communicate vital information accurately, collaborate with interdisciplinary teams, and engage in empathetic and compassionate conversations with patients and their families. Poor communication can lead to medical errors, misunderstandings, and compromised patient outcomes. Strong communication skills are essential for building trust, fostering patient satisfaction, and ensuring quality care.

Communication in Social and Cultural Contexts:

Communication is influenced by social and cultural factors, and understanding these nuances is vital for effective interaction. Cultural differences in communication styles, norms, and values can lead to misunderstandings or misinterpretations. Awareness of these differences allows individuals to adapt their communication strategies and avoid potential conflicts. In a globalized world, intercultural communication skills are increasingly important for fostering understanding and collaboration across diverse communities.

Benefits of Strong Communication Skills:

Developing strong communication skills brings numerous benefits. It enhances personal and professional relationships, improves teamwork and collaboration, and fosters trust and respect. Effective communication helps individuals express themselves with clarity, assertiveness, and confidence. It allows for better problem-solving, conflict resolution, and decision-making. Strong communicators are more likely to succeed in their careers, build meaningful connections, and navigate challenging situations with ease.

Conclusion:

Communication is the lifeblood of human interaction, serving as a bridge between individuals and facilitating the exchange of information, ideas, and emotions. Understanding the importance of communication is key to developing strong interpersonal skills and navigating various aspects of life successfully. By cultivating effective communication skills, individuals can enhance their personal relationships, thrive in the workplace, excel in education, and connect with others on a deeper level. Communication is an art worth mastering, and its power can shape lives and create a world where understanding and connection thrive.

Subchapter 2: Elements of Effective Communication

Introduction:

Effective communication involves much more than mere exchange of words. It encompasses various elements that work together to convey messages clearly, foster understanding, and establish meaningful connections. In this subchapter, we will explore the key elements of effective communication and how they contribute to successful interactions.

1. Clarity and Conciseness:

Clear and concise communication is essential for ensuring that the intended message is understood accurately. It involves organizing thoughts and ideas in a logical manner, using simple and straightforward language, and avoiding jargon or unnecessary complexity. Clarity helps to minimize misunderstandings, promotes transparency, and facilitates efficient information transfer.

2. Active Listening:

Effective communication is a two-way process that requires active listening. Active listening involves giving one's full attention to the speaker, seeking to understand their perspective, and responding appropriately. It requires focusing on the speaker's words, observing their nonverbal cues, and providing verbal or nonverbal feedback to demonstrate engagement and understanding.

3. Nonverbal Communication:

Nonverbal cues, such as body language, facial expressions, gestures, and tone of voice, play a significant role in communication. They can reinforce or contradict verbal messages, convey emotions, and provide additional context. Being aware of one's own nonverbal cues and interpreting those of others accurately enhances communication and helps to establish rapport and trust.

4. Empathy and Understanding:

Empathy is the ability to understand and share the feelings and perspectives of others. It is a crucial element of effective communication, as it enables individuals to connect on a deeper level and respond with compassion. By actively considering the emotions and experiences of others, communicators can foster empathy and create a safe and supportive environment for open dialogue.

5. Respect and Courtesy:

Respect and courtesy form the foundation of respectful communication. Treating others with respect, regardless of their background or opinions, helps to create a positive and inclusive communication environment. Politeness, active listening, and acknowledging the contributions of others demonstrate courtesy and contribute to productive and harmonious interactions.

6. Adaptability:

Effective communicators adapt their communication style to suit different situations, audiences, and contexts. They recognize that individuals have different communication preferences and adjust their approach accordingly. Adapting language, tone, and style to match the needs and expectations of the listener enhances understanding and promotes effective communication.

7. Feedback and Clarification:

Feedback is an essential element of effective communication. Providing feedback allows for clarification, affirmation, and constructive guidance. It helps to ensure that messages are understood correctly and promotes a continuous cycle of improvement. Seeking clarification when necessary also demonstrates a commitment to understanding and resolving any potential misunderstandings.

8. Timing and Relevance:

The timing and relevance of communication can significantly impact its effectiveness. Choosing the right moment to communicate and ensuring that the information is timely and pertinent to the situation or topic at hand improves the likelihood of successful communication. Understanding the context and adapting the timing and relevance of messages accordingly enhances their impact.

9. Confidence:

Confidence plays a vital role in effective communication. Communicators who exude confidence in their speech, body language, and overall demeanor inspire trust and credibility. Confidence allows individuals to express their thoughts and ideas assertively, navigate challenging conversations, and engage in effective persuasion or negotiation.

10. Emotional Intelligence:

Emotional intelligence is the ability to recognize and manage one's own emotions and understand the emotions of others. It enables individuals to navigate emotions in communication, respond empathetically, and adapt their communication approach based on emotional cues. Developing emotional intelligence enhances communication skills and fosters stronger connections with others.

Conclusion:

Effective communication encompasses various elements that work in harmony to ensure messages are conveyed clearly, understood accurately, and establish meaningful connections. By incorporating elements such as clarity, active listening, empathy, respect, adaptability, and emotional intelligence, individuals can become skilled communicators capable of fostering understanding, collaboration, and positive relationships.

Subchapter 3: Overcoming Communication Barriers

Introduction:

Despite our best efforts, communication barriers can arise and hinder effective understanding and connection. These barriers can be caused by various factors, including differences in language, culture, perception, and personal biases. In this subchapter, we will explore common communication barriers and discuss strategies to overcome them.

1. Language Barriers:

Language differences pose a significant communication barrier, particularly in multicultural and multilingual settings. To overcome this barrier, individuals can:

- Use simple and clear language.

- Avoid jargon and technical terms.

- Utilize visual aids, gestures, and body language to enhance understanding.

- Seek assistance from interpreters or translators when necessary.

- Invest time in language learning and cultural understanding to bridge gaps.

2. Cultural Barriers:

Cultural differences can lead to misunderstandings and misinterpretations in communication. To navigate cultural barriers effectively, individuals can:

- Be aware of cultural norms, values, and communication styles.

- Show respect and curiosity towards different cultures.

- Avoid making assumptions or generalizations.

- Seek clarification and ask open-ended questions to foster understanding.

- Embrace diversity and adapt communication approaches to accommodate cultural differences.

3. Perceptual Barriers:

Perception plays a crucial role in how we interpret and understand information. Perceptual barriers can arise due to differences in experiences, beliefs, and biases. To overcome perceptual barriers, individuals can:

- Practice active listening to genuinely understand others' perspectives.

- Avoid making judgments or assumptions based on personal biases.

- Seek clarification and ask for different viewpoints.

- Cultivate empathy and consider others' experiences and backgrounds.

- Recognize the limitations of one's own perception and remain open to new insights.

4. Emotional Barriers:

Emotions can impact communication by influencing how messages are received and interpreted. Emotional barriers may include anger, fear, anxiety, or defensiveness. To overcome emotional barriers, individuals can:

- Manage emotions effectively through self-awareness and regulation.

- Create a safe and supportive environment for open dialogue.

- Practice active listening and validate others' emotions.

- Use "I" statements to express thoughts and feelings constructively.

- Seek common ground and focus on solutions rather than dwelling on negative emotions.

5. Technological Barriers:

In today's digital age, communication often relies on technology, which can present its own set of challenges. To overcome technological barriers, individuals can:

- Ensure a stable and reliable internet connection for virtual communication.

- Familiarize themselves with communication platforms and tools.

- Use clear and concise language in written digital communication.

- Confirm receipt and understanding of messages to avoid misunderstandings.

- Employ video conferencing and screen sharing for more effective virtual communication.

6. Listening Barriers:

Poor listening skills can impede effective communication. To overcome listening barriers, individuals can:

- Practice active listening by giving full attention to the speaker.

- Avoid interrupting and allow others to express themselves fully.

- Ask clarifying questions to ensure understanding.

- Avoid distractions and create a conducive environment for listening.

- Practice empathy and try to understand the underlying messages and emotions.

7. Feedback and Communication Gap Barriers:

Inadequate or ineffective feedback can create a communication gap, hindering understanding and progress. To overcome feedback and communication gap barriers, individuals can:

- Provide specific, constructive, and timely feedback.

- Encourage open and honest communication.

- Seek feedback from others to gain different perspectives.

- Use active listening and paraphrasing to confirm understanding.

- Regularly check for feedback and ensure messages are received and interpreted correctly.

Conclusion:

Communication barriers are common, but they can be overcome with awareness, empathy, and effective strategies. By addressing language, cultural, perceptual, emotional, technological, listening, and feedback gaps, individuals can bridge communication barriers, foster understanding, and create meaningful connections. Overcoming these barriers contributes to improved relationships, increased collaboration, and enhanced personal and professional growth.

Chapter 2: The Art of Listening

Subchapter 1: Active Listening Techniques

Introduction:

Listening is a fundamental aspect of effective communication. Active listening goes beyond simply hearing words; it involves fully engaging with the speaker, understanding their message, and responding in a way that demonstrates attentiveness and comprehension. In this subchapter, we will explore active listening techniques and how they can enhance communication and foster meaningful connections.

1. Give Your Full Attention:

To actively listen, it is crucial to give your full attention to the speaker. Eliminate distractions and focus on the person speaking. Maintain eye contact, adopt an open body posture, and refrain from interrupting or multitasking. By demonstrating your undivided attention, you create a safe and supportive space for effective communication.

2. Practice Nonverbal Communication:

Nonverbal cues play a significant role in active listening. Use appropriate nonverbal signals to convey your engagement and understanding. Nodding, smiling, and maintaining an open and receptive facial expression can encourage the speaker to continue sharing their thoughts and feelings. Nonverbal cues also help to establish rapport and build trust.

3. Reflect and Paraphrase:

Reflecting and paraphrasing are techniques that show the speaker that you are actively listening and understanding their message. Reflecting involves summarizing or repeating key points to confirm your understanding. Paraphrasing goes a step further by restating the speaker's words in your own language, demonstrating empathy and ensuring accurate comprehension.

4. Ask Open-Ended Questions:

Asking open-ended questions encourages the speaker to provide more detailed and expansive responses. These questions cannot be answered with a simple "yes" or "no" and require the speaker to elaborate and share their thoughts and feelings. Open-ended questions promote deeper exploration of the topic and foster a more meaningful and engaging conversation.

5. Practice Empathy:

Empathy is the ability to understand and share the feelings and perspectives of others. When actively listening, put yourself in the speaker's shoes and try to genuinely understand their experiences and emotions. Show empathy through verbal and nonverbal cues, such as acknowledging their emotions, using supportive language, and responding with compassion.

6. Avoid Judgment and Assumptions:

Active listening requires an open and non-judgmental mindset. Avoid jumping to conclusions or making assumptions about the speaker's thoughts, intentions, or experiences. Suspend judgment and focus on understanding their perspective without imposing your own biases. This creates a safe and inclusive space for open communication.

7. Practice Mindfulness:

Mindfulness is the practice of being fully present and aware in the moment. Apply mindfulness principles to active listening by staying fully engaged and focused on the speaker. Be aware of your own thoughts and emotions that may arise during the conversation, but gently redirect your attention back to the speaker and their message.

8. Provide Feedback and Encouragement:

Offering feedback and encouragement demonstrates your active listening and engagement. Provide verbal cues, such as nodding, saying "yes" or "I understand," or using encouraging phrases like "Go on" or "Tell me more." This feedback encourages the speaker to continue sharing their thoughts and validates their contributions to the conversation.

9. Manage Your Response Time:

While actively listening, it is important to manage your response time effectively. Avoid interrupting the speaker and allow them to express themselves fully. Take brief pauses after the speaker finishes to ensure they have completed their thoughts before responding. This approach shows respect for their perspective and encourages open dialogue.

10. Reflect on Your Listening Skills:

Regularly reflect on your listening skills and identify areas for improvement. Consider seeking feedback from others to gain insight into how effectively you listen. Practice self-awareness and be mindful of any biases, distractions, or habits that may hinder your active listening. Continually strive to enhance your listening abilities.

Conclusion:

Active listening techniques are invaluable tools for effective communication. By giving your full attention, using nonverbal communication, reflecting and paraphrasing, asking open-ended questions, practicing empathy, avoiding judgment, being mindful, providing feedback, managing your response time, and reflecting on your listening skills, you can become a skilled and engaged listener. Active listening strengthens connections, fosters understanding, and promotes successful communication exchanges.

Subchapter 2: Empathetic Listening and its Impact

Introduction:

Empathetic listening is a powerful form of active listening that goes beyond understanding the speaker's words. It involves genuinely seeking to understand their emotions, perspectives, and experiences. Empathetic listening builds trust, strengthens relationships, and fosters a deeper level of connection. In this subchapter, we will explore empathetic listening and its profound impact on communication.

1. Understanding Emotions:

Empathetic listening involves recognizing and understanding the emotions expressed by the speaker. It requires actively listening for emotional cues in their tone of voice, body language, and choice of words. By acknowledging and validating their emotions, you create a supportive environment where they feel heard and understood.

2. Suspending Judgment:

Empathetic listening requires suspending judgment and setting aside preconceived notions or biases. It involves adopting an open and non-judgmental mindset to truly understand the speaker's perspective. By withholding judgment, you create a safe space for them to express themselves honestly and without fear of criticism.

3. Active Presence:

Being actively present is a crucial aspect of empathetic listening. It means giving your full attention to the speaker, both verbally and nonverbally. Maintain eye contact, use appropriate nonverbal cues to show engagement, and refrain from distractions or interruptions. By being fully present, you convey respect and demonstrate that their thoughts and feelings are valued.

4. Reflective Responses:

Empathetic listening involves providing reflective responses that demonstrate understanding and empathy. Reflective responses can include paraphrasing, summarizing, or rephrasing the speaker's words to ensure accurate comprehension. By reflecting back their thoughts and feelings, you validate their experiences and show that you are actively listening.

5. Cultivating Empathy:

Empathy is a key component of empathetic listening. It involves putting yourself in the speaker's shoes and seeking to understand their perspective and emotions. Cultivating empathy requires an open mind, a willingness to learn from others, and a genuine desire to connect on a deeper level. By practicing empathy, you create a sense of trust and foster a stronger bond with the speaker.

6. Creating a Safe Space:

Empathetic listening creates a safe space for open and honest communication. It encourages the speaker to share their thoughts, feelings, and experiences without fear of judgment or ridicule. By creating a non-threatening environment, you promote vulnerability and trust, allowing for meaningful and authentic conversations to take place.

7. Building Trust and Strengthening Relationships:

Empathetic listening builds trust and strengthens relationships. When individuals feel heard, understood, and valued, they develop a sense of trust in the listener. This trust forms the foundation for open communication, collaboration, and deeper connections. Empathetic listening nurtures positive relationships and creates a supportive network.

8. Problem Solving and Conflict Resolution:

Empathetic listening plays a vital role in problem-solving and conflict resolution. By truly understanding the emotions and perspectives of all parties involved, you can work towards finding mutually beneficial solutions. Empathetic listening helps to de-escalate conflicts, fosters empathy between individuals, and promotes effective resolution of issues.

9. Personal and Professional Growth:

Engaging in empathetic listening not only benefits the speaker but also contributes to personal and professional growth. By actively seeking to understand others and expanding your perspective, you gain insights and knowledge that can broaden your own understanding of the world. Empathetic listening enhances communication skills, emotional intelligence, and empathy, leading to personal development and growth.

10. Ripple Effect:

The impact of empathetic listening extends beyond the immediate conversation. When individuals experience empathetic listening, they are more likely to extend the same level of care and understanding to others. This creates a ripple effect, spreading empathy and fostering a culture of compassionate communication in various personal and professional interactions.

Conclusion:

Empathetic listening is a transformative skill that deepens connections, builds trust, and promotes understanding. By understanding emotions, suspending judgment, being actively present, providing reflective responses, cultivating empathy, creating a safe space, building trust, resolving conflicts, facilitating personal and professional growth, and generating a positive ripple effect, empathetic listening has a profound impact on communication and relationships.

Subchapter 3: Enhancing Listening Skills in Relationships

Introduction:

Effective listening is a crucial component of healthy and fulfilling relationships. It allows individuals to connect on a deeper level, understand each other's needs and desires, and foster trust and empathy. In this subchapter, we will explore strategies for enhancing listening skills specifically within the context of relationships.

1. Practice Active Listening:

Active listening is essential in relationships. Give your partner your full attention, maintain eye contact, and provide verbal and nonverbal cues to show that you are engaged in the conversation. Avoid distractions and genuinely focus on understanding their perspective. Active listening conveys respect and validates the importance of their words.

2. Validate Feelings:

When your partner shares their feelings, validate them by acknowledging and accepting their emotions. Avoid dismissing or belittling their feelings, even if you may not fully understand or agree with them. Validating feelings creates a safe space for open and honest communication, fostering emotional intimacy and trust.

3. Avoid Interrupting:

Interrupting can disrupt the flow of conversation and make your partner feel unheard. Practice restraint and let them express themselves fully before offering your response. Be patient and attentive, allowing them to communicate their thoughts and feelings without interruption. This demonstrates respect and shows that their words matter to you.

4. Show Empathy:

Empathy is vital in relationships. Make an effort to understand and empathize with your partner's experiences and emotions. Put yourself in their shoes and try to genuinely feel what they are feeling. Show empathy through supportive and understanding language, validating their perspective, and offering comfort when needed.

5. Ask Open-Ended Questions:

Asking open-ended questions encourages your partner to share more details and express themselves more fully. Instead of asking questions that can be answered with a simple "yes" or "no," ask questions that invite deeper reflection and elaboration. This allows for a richer and more meaningful exchange, leading to a better understanding of each other.

6. Reflect and Paraphrase:

Reflecting and paraphrasing are powerful techniques in enhancing listening skills within relationships. Repeat or summarize your partner's words to ensure accurate understanding. This not only shows that you are actively listening but also provides an opportunity for your partner to clarify or expand on their thoughts and feelings.

7. Be Non-Defensive:

When engaging in conversations with your partner, avoid becoming defensive. Instead of reacting with defensiveness or deflection, listen with an open mind and a willingness to understand their perspective. This fosters an environment where both partners feel safe to express themselves authentically, leading to more productive and constructive conversations.

8. Practice Mindful Listening:

Practice mindful listening by being fully present in the moment. Avoid distractions, set aside worries or preoccupations, and truly focus on your partner's words. Mindful listening allows you to notice subtle cues, both verbal and nonverbal, and to respond in a thoughtful and intentional manner.

9. Seek Clarification:

If you are unsure about something your partner said, seek clarification instead of making assumptions. Ask for more information or examples to ensure a clear understanding of their point. Clarification prevents misunderstandings and shows your commitment to actively listening and understanding their perspective.

10. Practice Regular Check-Ins:

Regularly check in with your partner to ensure that you are effectively listening and meeting each other's needs. Ask how they feel about your listening skills and if there are any areas for improvement. This open dialogue helps you continually enhance your listening abilities and strengthens your relationship.

Conclusion:

Enhancing listening skills within relationships is essential for building strong connections and fostering understanding. By practicing active listening, validating feelings, avoiding interruptions, showing empathy, asking open-ended questions, reflecting and paraphrasing, being non-defensive, practicing mindful listening, seeking clarification, and conducting regular check-ins, you can cultivate a healthy communication dynamic that promotes trust, empathy, and emotional intimacy within your relationship.

Chapter 3: Verbal Communication

Subchapter 1: The Power of Words

Introduction:

Verbal communication is a fundamental aspect of human interaction, shaping our relationships, influencing our perceptions, and conveying our thoughts and emotions. The words we choose and how we use them hold immense power. In this subchapter, we will explore the power of words and their impact on communication.

1. Words Shape Reality:

Words have the power to shape our reality. The language we use can influence how we perceive ourselves, others, and the world around us. Positive and empowering words can inspire confidence and foster a growth mindset, while negative or derogatory words can create self-doubt and perpetuate harmful beliefs. Being mindful of the words we use allows us to create a more positive and supportive communication environment.

2. Words Express Thoughts and Emotions:

Words serve as vehicles for expressing our thoughts and emotions. They allow us to articulate our ideas, share our experiences, and connect with others on a deeper level. By choosing our words carefully and expressing ourselves authentically, we can create meaningful connections and foster understanding in our interactions.

3. Words Have Emotional Impact:

The words we use have a profound emotional impact on ourselves and others. Positive and uplifting words can inspire joy, motivation, and encouragement, while negative or hurtful words can cause pain, frustration, and resentment. By being mindful of the emotional impact of our words, we can cultivate empathy, kindness, and emotional well-being in our communication.

4. Words Influence Perception:

Our choice of words can shape how others perceive us and interpret our messages. By using clear and concise language, we can convey our ideas effectively and minimize misunderstandings. Additionally, the tone, emphasis, and context in which we use words can significantly influence how our messages are received. Being aware of the potential interpretations of our words helps us communicate more intentionally.

5. Words Build or Break Relationships:

Words have the power to build or break relationships. Positive and affirming words can strengthen bonds, foster trust, and create a sense of belonging. On the other hand, negative or hurtful words can damage relationships, erode trust, and create distance between individuals. Choosing words that uplift, validate, and demonstrate respect is crucial for nurturing healthy and supportive relationships.

6. Words Drive Action:

The words we use can inspire action and drive change. Motivational and persuasive words have the ability to ignite passion, encourage collaboration, and mobilize individuals toward a common goal. By using words strategically, we can motivate others, inspire positive change, and contribute to personal and collective growth.

7. Words Facilitate Problem-Solving:

Effective problem-solving often relies on clear and constructive communication. By choosing words that promote understanding, active listening, and collaboration, we can navigate conflicts, resolve issues, and find mutually beneficial solutions. Using respectful and solution-focused language enhances the problem-solving process and encourages a cooperative mindset.

8. Words Reflect Our Values:

The words we use reflect our values, beliefs, and attitudes. By selecting words that align with our values, we can authentically express ourselves and cultivate meaningful connections with like-minded individuals. Consistency between our words and actions enhances credibility and fosters trust in our relationships.

9. Words Create Memorable Experiences:

Memorable experiences are often shaped by the words we encounter. Words have the ability to evoke emotions, spark inspiration, and leave a lasting impact. By using words that resonate with others, we can create meaningful and memorable experiences that enrich our relationships and leave a positive impression.

10. Words Have the Power to Heal:

Words have a healing power that can provide comfort, solace, and support during challenging times. Empathetic and compassionate words can offer reassurance, encouragement, and validation to those in need. By using words with kindness and empathy, we can provide a source of comfort and healing for ourselves and others.

Conclusion:

The power of words in verbal communication cannot be overstated. They shape our reality, express thoughts and emotions, have emotional impact, influence perception, build or break relationships, drive action, facilitate problem-solving, reflect our values, create memorable experiences, and have the power to heal. Being mindful of the words we choose and their impact allows us to harness the transformative power of language in our communication and create positive connections with others.

Subchapter 2: Effective Public Speaking Techniques

Introduction:

Public speaking is a valuable skill that allows individuals to communicate effectively and confidently in front of an audience. Whether it's delivering a presentation, giving a speech, or participating in a public forum, mastering effective public speaking techniques is essential. In this subchapter, we will explore techniques that can enhance your public speaking skills.

1. Preparation:

Effective public speaking begins with thorough preparation. Take the time to research and organize your content, ensuring that it flows logically and engages the audience. Prepare an outline or script, and practice your speech or presentation multiple times to build familiarity and confidence. Adequate preparation enables you to deliver your message with clarity and conviction.

2. Know Your Audience:

Understanding your audience is crucial for effective public speaking. Research the demographics, interests, and expectations of your audience beforehand. Tailor your content, language, and delivery style to resonate with their needs and interests. By connecting with your audience on a personal level, you can capture their attention and maintain their engagement throughout your presentation.

3. Engaging Opening:

Begin your speech or presentation with a strong and engaging opening. Grab the audience's attention with a compelling story, a thought-provoking question, a surprising fact, or a relevant anecdote. A captivating opening sets the tone for the rest of your presentation and piques the audience's curiosity, making them eager to hear more.

4. Clear Structure:

Maintain a clear and well-organized structure throughout your speech. Use an introduction to establish the purpose and outline of your presentation. Follow it with a coherent body that presents your main points and supporting evidence. Conclude with a concise summary that reinforces your key message and leaves a lasting impression. A clear structure helps the audience follow your thoughts and retain the information you present.

5. Use Visual Aids:

Visual aids, such as slides, props, or multimedia, can enhance your presentation and reinforce your message. Use visual aids sparingly and ensure they complement your speech rather than distract from it. Keep them simple, visually appealing, and easy to understand. Visual aids can help clarify complex information, engage visual learners, and make your presentation more memorable.

6. Use Body Language:

Your body language plays a significant role in public speaking. Maintain good posture, make eye contact with the audience, and use gestures to emphasize key points. Move naturally and purposefully on stage to command attention and display confidence. Your body language should align with your words, conveying authenticity and conviction.

7. Vocal Variety:

Varying your voice's tone, pitch, and pace adds depth and interest to your speech. Use pauses strategically to emphasize important points and allow the audience to absorb information. Speak clearly and audibly, ensuring that everyone in the audience can hear and understand you. Vocal variety captures attention, conveys enthusiasm, and keeps the audience engaged throughout your presentation.

8. Connect Emotionally:

Emotional connection is vital in public speaking. Inject emotion into your delivery by sharing personal stories, using vivid language, and evoking appropriate emotions through your words. Connect with the audience on an emotional level, helping them relate to your message and fostering a memorable experience. Authenticity and vulnerability can create a strong bond between you and the audience.

9. Handle Nervousness:

Nervousness is common when speaking in public. Acknowledge and embrace your nerves as a sign of excitement and readiness. Practice deep breathing and positive self-talk to calm your nerves. Visualize success and focus on delivering your message rather than on your anxiety. Remember that the audience wants you to succeed and is rooting for you.

10. Engage the Audience:

Engaging the audience is essential for effective public speaking. Involve them by asking rhetorical questions, incorporating interactive elements, or encouraging participation. Seek feedback, maintain eye contact, and be responsive to their reactions. Engaging the audience creates a dynamic and interactive experience, making your presentation more memorable and impactful.

Conclusion:

Mastering effective public speaking techniques is a valuable skill that can elevate your communication abilities. By preparing thoroughly, knowing your audience, delivering an engaging opening, maintaining a clear structure, using visual aids, utilizing body language, incorporating vocal variety, connecting emotionally, handling nervousness, and actively engaging the audience, you can deliver powerful and impactful speeches or presentations that leave a lasting impression. With practice and dedication, you can become a confident and persuasive public speaker.

Subchapter 3: Mastering the Art of Storytelling

Introduction:

Storytelling is a powerful tool that captivates audiences, conveys messages effectively, and connects people on an emotional level. Whether in public speaking, writing, or interpersonal communication, mastering the art of storytelling enhances your ability to engage, inspire, and influence others. In this subchapter, we will explore techniques to help you master the art of storytelling.

1. Identify Your Purpose:

Before crafting a story, clarify your purpose. Determine what message, lesson, or emotion you want to convey to your audience. Understanding your purpose helps you shape your story and select the most relevant details and themes to align with your desired outcome.

2. Structure Your Story:

Every compelling story has a clear structure. Begin with an engaging introduction that grabs the audience's attention and establishes the context. Develop the central plot, incorporating conflict, suspense, and resolution. Ensure a satisfying conclusion that ties all the elements together and leaves a lasting impact. A well-structured story keeps the audience engaged and invested in the narrative.

3. Create Vivid Characters:

Develop memorable characters in your story. Give them distinct personalities, motivations, and conflicts. The audience should be able to relate to or empathize with the characters, forming a connection that draws them deeper into the story. Use descriptive language and details to bring the characters to life and make them relatable.

4. Use Descriptive Language:

Effective storytelling relies on vivid and descriptive language. Paint a visual and sensory picture through your words, allowing the audience to immerse themselves in the story. Use metaphors, similes, and sensory details to evoke emotions and create a compelling atmosphere. Well-chosen descriptive language enhances the impact of your story.

5. Incorporate Emotion:

Emotions are a powerful driving force in storytelling. Engage your audience by tapping into their emotions. Make them feel joy, sadness, excitement, or empathy through the experiences of your characters. By connecting on an emotional level, your story becomes more relatable and memorable.

6. Show, Don't Tell:

Show, don't tell, is a golden rule in storytelling. Instead of simply stating facts or emotions, use descriptive scenes, dialogue, and actions to reveal them. Allow the audience to experience the story through their senses and draw their conclusions. Showing creates a more engaging and immersive experience for the audience.

7. Maintain a Compelling Pace:

Keep your story's pace engaging and balanced. Use a mix of slower, reflective moments and faster-paced, action-packed scenes. Build suspense, create tension, and vary the rhythm to maintain the audience's interest. A well-paced story keeps the audience eagerly anticipating what happens next.

8. Use Dialogue Effectively:

Dialogue brings characters to life and adds authenticity to your story. Use dialogue to reveal personalities, advance the plot, and convey emotions. Make the dialogue natural and engaging, reflecting the unique voices and perspectives of your characters. Dialogue adds depth and dynamics to your storytelling.

9. Utilize Humor:

Humor can be a powerful storytelling tool. Well-timed and appropriate humor lightens the mood, engages the audience, and helps them connect with the story. Incorporate humorous anecdotes, witty remarks, or clever wordplay to add levity and enhance the overall storytelling experience.

10. Practice and Refine:

Storytelling is an art that requires practice and refinement. Practice telling your stories aloud, paying attention to pacing, tone, and delivery. Seek feedback from trusted individuals and incorporate their suggestions to improve your storytelling skills. Continually refine your stories based on audience reactions and the desired impact.

Conclusion:

Mastering the art of storytelling is a valuable skill that enables you to captivate, inspire, and connect with your audience. By identifying your purpose, structuring your story, creating vivid characters, using descriptive language, incorporating emotion, showing instead of telling, maintaining a compelling pace, utilizing dialogue effectively, utilizing humor, and practicing and refining your storytelling abilities, you can become a skilled storyteller who leaves a lasting impression on your audience. With dedication and creativity, you can harness the power of storytelling to enhance your communication skills and make a meaningful impact.

Chapter 4: Nonverbal Communication

Subchapter 1: Understanding Body Language

Introduction:

Nonverbal communication, including body language, plays a significant role in how we convey messages, express emotions, and establish connections with others. Understanding and interpreting body language can enhance our communication skills and provide valuable insights into unspoken cues. In this subchapter, we will explore the importance of body language and how to understand its various aspects.

1. The Role of Body Language:

Body language refers to the nonverbal signals we send through facial expressions, gestures, posture, eye contact, and other physical cues. It complements and often reinforces our verbal communication, conveying additional meaning and providing context to our words. Being aware of body language helps us understand others better and allows us to communicate more effectively.

2. Facial Expressions:

Facial expressions are one of the most important aspects of body language. Our faces convey a wide range of emotions, such as happiness, sadness, anger, surprise, and disgust. Understanding and interpreting facial expressions can provide valuable insights into a person's feelings and intentions. Pay attention to the movements of the eyebrows, eyes, mouth, and overall expression to gain a deeper understanding of someone's emotional state.

3. Gestures and Hand Movements:

Gestures and hand movements can convey a wealth of information. They can emphasize or clarify verbal messages, indicate directions, illustrate concepts, or express emotions. Different cultures may have distinct meanings associated with specific gestures, so it's important to be mindful of cultural differences when interpreting gestures. Pay attention to the direction, intensity, and context of hand movements to better understand their intended message.

4. Posture and Body Alignment:

Posture and body alignment can reveal a lot about a person's confidence, attitude, and emotional state. A slouched posture may indicate low self-esteem or disinterest, while an upright and open posture conveys confidence and engagement. Pay attention to the alignment of the body, head, and shoulders to gauge a person's level of attentiveness and receptiveness.

5. Eye Contact:

Eye contact is a powerful nonverbal cue that can communicate interest, attention, sincerity, and confidence. Maintaining appropriate eye contact during a conversation conveys respect and shows that you are actively engaged. However, it's important to consider cultural norms, as the level of eye contact may vary across different cultures.

6. Proxemics:

Proxemics refers to the study of personal space and the distance we maintain between ourselves and others during communication. Different cultures have different norms regarding personal space, and violating these norms can make people feel uncomfortable or intruded upon. Pay attention to the distance between individuals and adjust accordingly to respect personal boundaries.

7. Microexpressions:

Microexpressions are brief, involuntary facial expressions that occur within a fraction of a second. They can reveal genuine emotions that someone may be trying to conceal or downplay. Being able to detect microexpressions can provide valuable insights into a person's true feelings and intentions. Look for subtle changes in the face, such as fleeting expressions of surprise, fear, or contempt.

8. Vocal Tone and Inflection:

While not strictly body language, vocal tone and inflection are important aspects of nonverbal communication. The way we speak, including the pitch, volume, rhythm, and emphasis, can convey emotions, attitudes, and intentions. Pay attention to vocal cues to gain a deeper understanding of the underlying messages being conveyed.

9. Congruence and Incongruence:

In nonverbal communication, congruence refers to the alignment between verbal and nonverbal cues, while incongruence occurs when there is a mismatch between them. Pay attention to inconsistencies between what someone is saying and their body language. Incongruence can indicate discomfort, deception, or conflicting emotions.

10. Cultural Considerations:

It's essential to recognize that body language cues can vary across cultures. Different cultures have distinct norms and interpretations of nonverbal signals. Be sensitive to cultural differences and adapt your understanding of body language accordingly to avoid misunderstandings.

Conclusion:

Understanding body language is crucial for effective communication. By paying attention to facial expressions, gestures, posture, eye contact, vocal cues, and cultural considerations, we can gain valuable insights into a person's emotions, attitudes, and intentions. Developing proficiency in interpreting body language allows us to communicate more effectively, build rapport, and establish stronger connections with others.

Subchapter 2: The Role of Facial Expressions and Gestures

Introduction:

Facial expressions and gestures are powerful forms of nonverbal communication that can convey a wealth of information and greatly enhance our understanding of others. In this subchapter, we will explore the role of facial expressions and gestures in communication and how to interpret their meanings.

1. Facial Expressions:

Facial expressions are a primary means of conveying emotions and feelings. The face is highly expressive, with various muscles working together to form different expressions. Some commonly recognized facial expressions include happiness, sadness, anger, surprise, fear, and disgust. By observing someone's facial expressions, we can gain insights into their emotional state and gauge their reactions to a given situation.

2. Microexpressions:

Microexpressions are subtle, fleeting facial expressions that occur involuntarily and often go unnoticed. They can reveal true emotions that someone may be trying to hide or suppress. Paying attention to microexpressions can provide valuable cues about a person's true feelings and intentions. These microexpressions typically last for just a fraction of a second, so keen observation and attentiveness are essential for detecting them.

3. Gestures:

Gestures are movements of the hands, arms, or body that accompany verbal communication and add meaning to the message being conveyed. They can be used to emphasize key points, illustrate concepts, or express emotions. Different gestures can have different meanings across cultures, so it's important to be mindful of cultural variations when interpreting gestures. Common gestures include pointing, nodding, shaking the head, thumbs up, and handshakes.

4. Emblematic Gestures:

Emblematic gestures are specific hand movements or gestures that carry a recognized meaning within a particular culture or group. These gestures can be used to replace or reinforce verbal messages. Examples of emblematic gestures include the peace sign, thumbs up, waving goodbye, and the OK sign. Understanding emblematic gestures can help us interpret nonverbal cues more accurately and avoid misunderstandings.

5. Illustrators:

Illustrators are gestures that accompany and enhance verbal communication. They are used to visually illustrate or emphasize key points. For example, using hand movements to demonstrate the size or shape of an object, or using gestures to depict a sequence of events. Illustrators can help make communication more engaging, memorable, and effective.

6. Adaptors:

Adaptors are self-touching or self-manipulating gestures that individuals use to alleviate stress, anxiety, or discomfort. These gestures are often unconscious and can include actions such as touching the face, fidgeting, or playing with objects. Adaptors can provide insights into a person's level of nervousness or unease. However, it's important to note that adaptors alone are not always indicative of deception or discomfort, and they should be considered in conjunction with other nonverbal cues.

7. Cultural Differences:

It's crucial to recognize that facial expressions and gestures can vary across cultures. Different cultures may have distinct interpretations and meanings associated with specific facial expressions and gestures. Gestures that are considered acceptable or polite in one culture may be offensive or inappropriate in another. When interpreting facial expressions and gestures, it's essential to be aware of and respect cultural differences to avoid miscommunication.

8. Context and Congruence:

When interpreting facial expressions and gestures, it's important to consider the context in which they occur. The meaning of a facial expression or gesture can vary depending on the situation, relationship dynamics, and cultural context. Additionally, it's essential to look for congruence between facial expressions, gestures, and verbal communication. Consistency between verbal and nonverbal cues enhances the accuracy of interpretation.

9. Active Observation and Practice:

To improve your ability to interpret facial expressions and gestures, practice active observation in various social interactions. Pay attention to the subtleties of facial expressions and gestures, and compare them to the verbal messages being conveyed. Over time, with practice and increased awareness, you can become more skilled at understanding and interpreting nonverbal cues.

Conclusion:

Facial expressions and gestures are powerful forms of nonverbal communication that significantly contribute to our understanding of others. By observing and interpreting facial expressions and gestures, we can gain insights into a person's emotions, attitudes, and intentions. However, it's important to consider cultural variations, context, and the congruence between verbal and nonverbal cues. By honing our observation skills and practicing active interpretation, we can become more proficient in understanding the role of facial expressions and gestures in communication.

Subchapter 3: Using Nonverbal Cues to Enhance Communication

Introduction:

Nonverbal cues play a vital role in communication, allowing us to convey meaning, emotions, and intentions beyond words. In this subchapter, we will explore how to use nonverbal cues effectively to enhance our communication skills and create stronger connections with others.

1. Body Language and Presence:

Your body language and presence can significantly impact how others perceive and respond to your communication. Maintain an open and relaxed posture, make appropriate eye contact, and use facial expressions that align with your message. Nonverbal cues such as a confident stance and attentive body language help establish trust and engagement.

2. Active Listening Nonverbal Cues:

Nonverbal cues are instrumental in demonstrating active listening. Use nodding, leaning forward slightly, and maintaining eye contact to show that you are fully present and attentive. These cues signal that you value the speaker's words and encourage them to continue sharing their thoughts.

3. Mirroring and Matching:

Mirroring and matching nonverbal cues can foster rapport and connection with others. Subtly align your body language, gestures, and even vocal tone with those of the person you are communicating with. This technique helps create a sense of familiarity and understanding, making the conversation more comfortable and harmonious.

4. Gestures and Visual Aids:

Incorporating gestures and visual aids can enhance your verbal communication and make your message more engaging and memorable. Use hand gestures to emphasize key points, illustrate concepts, or add visual variety to your presentation. Visual aids such as charts, diagrams, or props can further support your message and provide visual reinforcement.

5. Tone and Inflection:

Your vocal tone and inflection are crucial nonverbal cues that convey meaning and emotions. Use variations in tone, pitch, and pace to emphasize important points, convey enthusiasm, or express empathy. A well-modulated voice adds depth and clarity to your verbal communication, enhancing the overall impact of your message.

6. Proxemics and Personal Space:

Be mindful of proxemics, which refers to the use of personal space during communication. Respect others' personal space by maintaining an appropriate distance, considering cultural norms and individual preferences. Invading personal space can create discomfort and hinder effective communication.

7. Facial Expressions and Emotional Contagion:

Facial expressions are powerful nonverbal cues that can elicit emotional responses from others. Be aware of your facial expressions and aim to convey positive emotions such as warmth, empathy, and sincerity. Smiling and showing genuine interest through facial expressions can create a positive atmosphere and promote emotional contagion, where others mirror your emotions and become more receptive to your message.

8. Silence and Pauses:

Silence and well-placed pauses are nonverbal cues that can enhance communication. Use intentional silence to allow for reflection, emphasize a point, or signal a transition. Pausing also gives others the opportunity to process information or contribute to the conversation, fostering a more inclusive and interactive exchange.

9. Nonverbal Cues in Cross-Cultural Communication:

When communicating across cultures, be aware of cultural differences in nonverbal cues. Different cultures may interpret body language, gestures, and expressions differently. Educate yourself about cultural norms and adapt your nonverbal communication style to ensure effective cross-cultural understanding and respect.

10. Practice and Feedback:

Enhancing nonverbal communication skills takes practice. Pay attention to your own nonverbal cues, observe others' responses, and seek feedback from trusted individuals. Continuously refine and adjust your nonverbal communication to build stronger connections and improve your overall communication effectiveness.

Conclusion:

Using nonverbal cues effectively can significantly enhance your communication skills and foster stronger connections with others. By being mindful of your body language, active listening cues, mirroring, gestures, vocal tone, and cultural considerations, you can create a positive and engaging communication experience. Regular practice and feedback will further refine your nonverbal communication abilities, leading to more impactful and successful interactions.

Chapter 5: Communication Styles and Strategies

Subchapter 1: Assertive Communication and Conflict Resolution

Introduction:

Effective communication involves navigating different communication styles and resolving conflicts in a constructive manner. In this subchapter, we will explore assertive communication and conflict resolution strategies that promote understanding, collaboration, and positive outcomes.

1. Understanding Assertive Communication:

Assertive communication is a style that involves expressing your thoughts, feelings, and needs in a respectful and direct manner, while also considering the rights and perspectives of others. It emphasizes clear and honest communication without being aggressive or passive. Assertive communicators express themselves confidently, assert their boundaries, and actively listen to others.

2. Benefits of Assertive Communication:

Assertive communication fosters open dialogue, promotes mutual understanding, and builds healthy relationships. It allows individuals to express their thoughts and emotions honestly and respectfully, leading to effective problem-solving and conflict resolution. Assertive communicators are more likely to be heard, understood, and respected by others.

3. Key Elements of Assertive Communication:

a. Clear and Direct Expression: Clearly state your thoughts, feelings, and needs using straightforward language, avoiding ambiguity or hints.

b. Active Listening: Listen attentively to others, acknowledge their perspectives, and demonstrate understanding.

c. Body Language and Tone: Use confident body language, maintain appropriate eye contact, and use a calm and assertive tone of voice.

d. Asserting Boundaries: Clearly define and assert your boundaries while respecting the boundaries of others.

e. "I" Statements: Use "I" statements to express your thoughts and feelings, taking ownership of your perspective rather than blaming others.

f. Problem-Solving Mindset: Focus on finding solutions and reaching mutual agreements rather than dwelling on the problem itself.

4. Conflict Resolution Strategies:

a. Identify the Issue: Clearly define the conflict and understand the underlying concerns or needs of all parties involved.

b. Active Listening: Actively listen to each other's perspectives without interruption, seeking to understand rather than respond.

c. Collaborative Problem-Solving: Encourage a collaborative approach to finding a solution that satisfies the needs of all parties involved.

d. Win-Win Approach: Strive for a win-win outcome where both parties feel their concerns are addressed and a mutually beneficial resolution is achieved.

e. Negotiation and Compromise: Identify areas of flexibility and willingness to compromise to find a middle ground.

f. Focus on Interests, Not Positions: Look beyond positions and understand the underlying interests and motivations of each party.

g. Seek Mediation if Necessary: In situations where resolution seems challenging, consider involving a neutral third party to facilitate communication and guide the conflict resolution process.

5. Emotional Intelligence in Conflict Resolution:

Emotional intelligence plays a crucial role in conflict resolution. It involves recognizing and managing your emotions and understanding the emotions of others. By practicing empathy, staying calm, and regulating your emotional responses, you can navigate conflicts with greater understanding and empathy.

6. Practice and Self-Reflection:

Developing assertive communication and conflict resolution skills requires practice and self-reflection. Engage in role-playing exercises, seek feedback from others, and reflect on your communication experiences to identify areas for improvement. Continuously work on enhancing your assertiveness and conflict resolution abilities.

Conclusion:

Assertive communication and effective conflict resolution are essential skills for fostering healthy relationships and productive interactions. By embracing assertive communication principles and employing conflict resolution strategies, individuals can express their needs, resolve conflicts constructively, and cultivate a positive communication environment. With practice, self-reflection, and a focus on understanding, individuals can develop stronger communication skills and build more harmonious connections with others.

Subchapter 2: Adapting Communication Styles to Different Audiences

Introduction:

Adapting your communication style to suit different audiences is essential for effective and successful communication. In this subchapter, we will explore strategies for adjusting your communication approach to connect with diverse audiences and ensure your message is understood and well-received.

1. Audience Analysis:

Before communicating with a particular audience, conduct an audience analysis to gather information about their demographics, background, knowledge level, and communication preferences. This analysis helps you tailor your message and select appropriate language, tone, and delivery methods.

2. Language and Terminology:

Choose language and terminology that are appropriate and understandable to your specific audience. Avoid using technical jargon or complex terms that may confuse or alienate listeners. Adapt your vocabulary to match the knowledge and expertise of your audience, ensuring they can easily grasp and relate to your message.

3. Tone and Style:

Consider the tone and style of your communication based on the audience's preferences and expectations. Adapt your tone to match the formality or informality of the situation. For example, a more casual and conversational tone may be suitable for a friendly gathering, while a more formal and professional tone may be appropriate for a business presentation.

4. Visual Aids and Examples:

Utilize visual aids and relatable examples to enhance understanding and engagement. Visuals such as charts, diagrams, or multimedia presentations can help clarify complex concepts and make your message more accessible. Incorporating relevant examples that resonate with your audience's experiences or interests can also improve comprehension and connection.

5. Delivery Method:

Consider the most effective delivery method for your audience. Some individuals may prefer face-to-face interactions, while others may respond better to written communication or digital platforms. Adapt your delivery method to match the preferences and accessibility of your audience, ensuring they can engage with your message comfortably.

6. Active Listening and Feedback:

Engage in active listening and encourage feedback from your audience to gauge their understanding and address any concerns or questions. Actively listen to their responses, demonstrate empathy, and be open to adjusting your communication style based on their feedback. This two-way communication approach strengthens the connection and promotes effective understanding.

7. Cultural Sensitivity:

Be mindful of cultural differences and adapt your communication style to respect and accommodate diverse cultural backgrounds. Different cultures may have unique communication norms, nonverbal cues, and sensitivities. Educate yourself about cultural considerations to avoid misunderstandings or inadvertently causing offense.

8. Flexibility and Adaptability:

Remain flexible and adaptable in your communication style. Different audiences may require different approaches, and being open to adjusting your style allows for effective communication in various contexts. Pay attention to the audience's reactions and adapt accordingly to maintain engagement and comprehension.

9. Empathy and Connection:

Demonstrate empathy and seek to establish a genuine connection with your audience. Consider their perspectives, emotions, and needs when tailoring your communication. Showing empathy and creating a sense of connection fosters trust, enhances rapport, and increases the likelihood of effective communication.

10. Continuous Learning and Improvement:

Continuously seek opportunities to learn and improve your communication skills. Reflect on your experiences, seek feedback, and engage in self-development to refine your ability to adapt your communication style to different audiences. Embrace a growth mindset and be open to learning from each interaction.

Conclusion:

Adapting your communication style to different audiences is crucial for successful and impactful communication. By conducting audience analysis, selecting appropriate language and tone, utilizing visual aids, and considering cultural sensitivities, you can connect with diverse audiences effectively. Embrace flexibility, active listening, empathy, and continuous learning to continuously refine your communication skills and build meaningful connections with others.

Subchapter 3: Building Rapport and Influence through Communication

Introduction:

Building rapport and influence through communication is essential for establishing strong relationships, gaining trust, and effectively conveying your ideas. In this subchapter, we will explore strategies for fostering rapport and influence through your communication style.

1. Active Listening:

Active listening is a fundamental component of building rapport. Pay attention to the speaker, maintain eye contact, and demonstrate genuine interest in what they have to say. Show empathy, ask clarifying questions, and paraphrase to ensure accurate understanding. Active listening conveys respect, validates others' perspectives, and fosters a sense of connection.

2. Authenticity:

Be authentic in your communication. Genuine and transparent communication helps build trust and credibility. Avoid pretenses or trying to be someone you're not. Be true to your values, beliefs, and personality. Authenticity enables others to relate to you on a deeper level, establishing a foundation for rapport and influence.

3. Empathy and Emotional Intelligence:

Develop empathy and emotional intelligence to better understand and connect with others. Put yourself in their shoes, acknowledge their emotions, and respond with empathy and understanding. Recognize and manage your own emotions, as well as read and respond to the emotional cues of others. Empathy creates a safe and supportive environment, enhancing rapport and influence.

4. Establish Common Ground:

Find common ground with your audience to establish rapport. Identify shared interests, experiences, or goals that you can relate to and discuss. Building on commonalities creates a sense of connection, mutual understanding, and trust. It allows you to communicate from a shared perspective, increasing your influence.

5. Nonverbal Communication:

Pay attention to your nonverbal communication, as it significantly influences how others perceive you. Maintain appropriate body language, use facial expressions that align with your message, and be mindful of your tone of voice. Nonverbal cues should complement and reinforce your verbal communication, conveying sincerity, confidence, and respect.

6. Clear and Concise Communication:

Ensure your message is clear, concise, and easily understandable. Use language that is appropriate for your audience and avoid jargon or complex terminology that may confuse or alienate them. Organize your thoughts effectively and deliver your message in a straightforward manner. Clear and concise communication enhances your influence by making your ideas more accessible and compelling.

7. Storytelling:

Utilize storytelling techniques to captivate your audience and make your message more relatable and memorable. Share personal anecdotes or use case studies that illustrate your points and evoke emotions. Storytelling helps engage the audience on an emotional level, fosters connections, and enhances your influence.

8. Building Trust:

Trust is crucial for building rapport and influence. Be reliable, follow through on commitments, and maintain confidentiality when necessary. Demonstrate competence and expertise in your communication. Trust is built over time through consistent and honest interactions, and it significantly impacts your ability to influence others.

9. Flexibility and Adaptability:

Adapt your communication style to different individuals and situations. Recognize and respect the preferences, communication styles, and cultural backgrounds of others. Flexibility allows you to connect with a diverse range of people and adapt your message to resonate with them, increasing your influence.

10. Continued Relationship Building:

Building rapport and influence is an ongoing process. Invest time and effort in nurturing relationships, maintaining regular communication, and showing genuine interest in others. Engage in active networking, seek opportunities to collaborate, and provide support when needed. Continued relationship building enhances your influence and expands your network.

Conclusion:

Building rapport and influence through communication requires active listening, authenticity, empathy, and clear communication. Establishing common ground, utilizing nonverbal cues, storytelling, and building trust are also key components. Adaptability, ongoing relationship building, and a focus on adding value to others contribute to your ability to influence and positively impact those around you. By incorporating these strategies into your communication approach, you can build strong connections, foster influence, and achieve your desired outcomes.

Chapter 6: Interpersonal Relationships

Subchapter 1: Effective Communication in Personal Relationships

Introduction:

Effective communication is vital for establishing and maintaining healthy and fulfilling interpersonal relationships. In this subchapter, we will explore strategies for fostering effective communication within personal relationships, promoting understanding, empathy, and connection.

1. Active Listening:

Active listening is a cornerstone of effective communication in personal relationships. Give your full attention to the speaker, maintain eye contact, and genuinely listen to their thoughts, feelings, and concerns. Practice empathy, ask open-ended questions, and provide validation to show that you value their perspective. Active listening creates a safe and supportive space for open and honest communication.

2. Open and Honest Expression:

Encourage open and honest expression within your personal relationships. Create an environment where individuals feel comfortable sharing their thoughts, emotions, and needs without fear of judgment or criticism. Foster trust by demonstrating that you are receptive to their perspective and committed to understanding them fully.

3. Emotional Intelligence:

Develop emotional intelligence to navigate and respond effectively to the emotions within personal relationships. Understand and manage your own emotions, as well as recognize and empathize with the emotions of others. Practice self-awareness, emotional regulation, and effective emotional expression to foster emotional connection and understanding.

4. Nonviolent Communication:

Utilize nonviolent communication techniques to promote understanding and resolve conflicts peacefully within personal relationships. Focus on expressing observations, feelings, needs, and requests in a non-judgmental and compassionate manner. Avoid blame or criticism and instead aim for mutual understanding and collaborative problem-solving.

5. Respectful Communication:

Maintain respect and kindness in your communication with loved ones. Use language that is considerate and affirming, even during moments of disagreement. Avoid disrespectful language, personal attacks, or belittling remarks that can erode trust and intimacy. Foster a culture of respect and acceptance within your personal relationships.

6. Conflict Resolution Skills:

Develop effective conflict resolution skills to address disagreements and conflicts constructively. Practice active listening, seek to understand the underlying concerns of all parties involved, and focus on finding mutually beneficial solutions. Use "I" statements to express your feelings and needs, and engage in collaborative problem-solving to reach resolutions that satisfy everyone involved.

7. Mindful Communication:

Practice mindful communication within personal relationships. Be present in your interactions, give your full attention, and avoid distractions. Mindfulness allows you to listen and respond attentively, fostering deeper connections and preventing misunderstandings. Cultivate a sense of mindfulness through meditation, self-reflection, and intentional communication practices.

8. Empathy and Validation:

Demonstrate empathy and validation towards your loved ones. Seek to understand their experiences, emotions, and perspectives. Show genuine care and compassion, and validate their feelings and experiences, even if you may not agree with them. Empathy and validation enhance emotional connection and trust within personal relationships.

9. Effective Use of Technology:

In the digital age, the effective use of technology can support communication within personal relationships. Utilize messaging platforms, video calls, and social media to stay connected and maintain ongoing communication. However, be mindful of the potential pitfalls, such as misinterpretation of tone or excessive reliance on digital communication. Strive to balance technology use with in-person interactions.

10. Continued Nurturing of Relationships:

Recognize that personal relationships require ongoing nurturing and effort. Dedicate time and energy to connect, communicate, and strengthen your relationships. Regularly check in with your loved ones, express appreciation, and engage in activities that foster shared experiences. Continued investment in relationships cultivates depth, trust, and long-lasting connection.

Conclusion:

Effective communication is the lifeblood of personal relationships, fostering understanding, empathy, and connection. By practicing active listening, open and honest expression, emotional intelligence, and respectful communication, you can enhance the quality of your relationships.

Employ conflict resolution skills, mindful communication, empathy, and validation to deepen emotional bonds. Embrace technology while maintaining a focus on in-person connections. Through ongoing nurturing and effort, personal relationships can thrive and bring fulfillment to your life.

Subchapter 2: Nurturing Professional Relationships

Introduction:

Building and nurturing professional relationships is essential for career success, collaboration, and personal growth. In this subchapter, we will explore strategies for effectively nurturing professional relationships through communication and fostering a positive work environment.

1. Networking:

Networking is a key aspect of nurturing professional relationships. Attend industry events, conferences, and seminars to connect with professionals in your field. Actively engage in networking opportunities, both online and offline, to expand your professional circle. Build genuine connections, exchange ideas, and offer support to cultivate meaningful relationships.

2. Relationship Building:

Invest time and effort in building relationships with colleagues, mentors, and supervisors. Engage in informal conversations, show genuine interest in their work, and seek opportunities for collaboration. Build rapport and trust by being reliable, respectful, and supportive. By fostering positive relationships, you create a strong professional network that can support your growth and advancement.

3. Effective Communication:

Effective communication is crucial for nurturing professional relationships. Be clear, concise, and professional in your written and verbal communication. Use active listening skills to understand others' perspectives and demonstrate empathy. Respond promptly to emails and messages, and be mindful of tone and language to maintain positive interactions.

4. Collaboration and Teamwork:

Collaboration and teamwork are essential for nurturing professional relationships in a work environment. Seek opportunities to work with colleagues on projects, contribute ideas, and support team goals. Foster a spirit of collaboration by promoting open communication, recognizing others' contributions, and celebrating team achievements. Strong teamwork builds trust and fosters positive relationships among colleagues.

5. Professional Development:

Invest in your own professional development to strengthen relationships in your field. Attend workshops, training programs, and seminars to expand your knowledge and skills. Share your learnings and insights with others, and seek feedback and mentorship from experienced professionals. Demonstrating a commitment to growth and improvement helps foster respect and credibility among your peers.

6. Recognition and Appreciation:

Recognize and appreciate the contributions of your colleagues and team members. Offer genuine praise and recognition for their achievements and efforts. Express gratitude for their support and assistance. Celebrate milestones and successes together to create a positive work environment that values and uplifts its members.

7. Conflict Resolution:

Handle conflicts professionally and constructively when they arise. Practice active listening, seek to understand all perspectives, and find mutually agreeable solutions. Address conflicts promptly and privately, emphasizing open communication and a desire for resolution. Effective conflict resolution demonstrates respect, problem-solving skills, and a commitment to maintaining positive professional relationships.

8. Mentorship and Mentoring Others:

Engage in mentorship relationships to foster professional growth and establish valuable connections. Seek mentors who can provide guidance, share their expertise, and offer career advice. Additionally, consider mentoring others and sharing your knowledge and experiences. Mentoring cultivates mutually beneficial relationships and contributes to a supportive professional network.

9. Professional Boundaries:

Maintain professional boundaries while nurturing relationships. Be mindful of confidentiality, respect personal space, and avoid engaging in gossip or office politics. Balance friendliness with professionalism to ensure that relationships remain focused on work-related goals and objectives.

10. Continued Relationship Maintenance:

Nurturing professional relationships requires ongoing effort. Schedule regular check-ins with colleagues and mentors, both in person and virtually. Stay connected through professional networking platforms and social media. Attend industry events and seminars to reconnect with contacts and expand your network. Continually investing in relationship maintenance strengthens professional connections over time.

Conclusion:

Nurturing professional relationships is essential for career growth and personal success. By networking, building relationships, communicating effectively, collaborating, and resolving conflicts professionally, you can foster a positive work environment and establish a strong professional network. Embrace ongoing professional development, recognition, mentorship, and the maintenance of boundaries to ensure the longevity and quality of your professional relationships.

Subchapter 3: Communication Skills for Successful Networking

Introduction:

Networking plays a crucial role in career advancement and professional growth. Effective communication skills are essential for successful networking, enabling you to connect with others, build relationships, and create opportunities. In this subchapter, we will explore communication skills that can enhance your networking success.

1. Elevator Pitch:

Craft a concise and compelling elevator pitch that introduces yourself and communicates your professional value. Your elevator pitch should summarize who you are, what you do, and what sets you apart. Practice delivering it with confidence and clarity to make a strong first impression when networking.

2. Active Listening:

Practice active listening when engaging in networking conversations. Give your full attention to the person you're speaking with, maintain eye contact, and demonstrate genuine interest in what they have to say. Ask open-ended questions to encourage further discussion and show that you value their perspective. Active listening helps build rapport and fosters meaningful connections.

3. Effective Verbal Communication:

Develop strong verbal communication skills for networking interactions. Speak clearly, enunciate your words, and use appropriate language and tone. Be concise and to the point while conveying your ideas effectively. Avoid jargon or technical terms that may confuse the listener. Practice articulating your thoughts and presenting yourself professionally.

4. Nonverbal Communication:

Pay attention to your nonverbal communication during networking interactions. Maintain good posture, use appropriate hand gestures, and exhibit open body language. Smile genuinely and maintain eye contact to convey interest and approachability. Your nonverbal cues should align with your verbal communication to create a positive impression.

5. Building Rapport:

Building rapport is crucial for successful networking. Find common ground and shared interests with the person you're speaking with. Show genuine curiosity and empathy towards their experiences and perspectives. Use mirroring techniques, such as matching their body language and tone, to establish rapport and create a sense of connection.

6. Follow-up Communication:

After networking events or conversations, follow up with individuals you've connected with. Send personalized emails or messages to express your appreciation for the conversation and to further the relationship. Demonstrate your interest in maintaining contact and explore potential collaboration or future discussions. Timely and thoughtful follow-up communication helps solidify the connection.

7. Networking Etiquette:

Be mindful of networking etiquette when engaging with professionals. Respect others' time and be considerate of their boundaries. Avoid monopolizing conversations or focusing solely on self-promotion. Instead, aim for a balanced and mutually beneficial exchange of ideas and information. Show gratitude and respect for the networking opportunities you encounter.

8. Authenticity:

Authenticity is key in networking interactions. Be genuine, transparent, and true to yourself. Avoid adopting a persona or pretending to be someone you're not. Authenticity helps build trust and fosters genuine connections. By being true to who you are, you attract individuals who resonate with your values and goals.

9. Relationship Building Mindset:

Approach networking with a mindset of building relationships rather than solely seeking immediate benefits. Focus on establishing meaningful connections and providing value to others. Offer assistance, share knowledge, and connect individuals who could benefit from each other's expertise. A relationship-building mindset leads to long-term connections and opportunities.

10. Continuous Networking:

Networking is an ongoing process, not just a one-time event. Continuously seek opportunities to expand your network and engage with professionals in your field. Attend industry conferences, join professional associations, and participate in networking events. Embrace networking as a continuous practice for professional growth.

Conclusion:

Effective communication skills are essential for successful networking. By honing your elevator pitch, practicing active listening, mastering verbal and nonverbal communication, building rapport, and following up with sincerity, you can enhance your networking success. Embrace authenticity, networking etiquette, a relationship-building mindset, and a continuous networking approach to forge meaningful professional connections that can open doors to new opportunities.

Chapter 7: Cultural Awareness and Communication

Subchapter 1: Understanding Cultural Differences in Communication

Introduction:

In today's globalized world, effective communication across cultures is essential for building strong relationships and fostering understanding. In this subchapter, we will explore the importance of cultural awareness in communication and examine how cultural differences impact our interactions.

1. Cultural Sensitivity:

Develop cultural sensitivity by acknowledging and respecting the diverse values, beliefs, customs, and communication styles of different cultures. Recognize that cultural norms and practices can significantly influence communication patterns and behaviors. Approach cross-cultural interactions with an open mind and a willingness to learn and adapt.

2. Verbal Communication Styles:

Different cultures may have distinct verbal communication styles. Some cultures may value direct and explicit communication, while others emphasize indirect and implicit communication. Understanding these differences can prevent misunderstandings and promote effective communication. Adapt your communication style by considering the cultural context and preferences of the individuals you are interacting with.

3. Nonverbal Communication:

Nonverbal communication cues, such as body language, facial expressions, and gestures, vary across cultures. It's crucial to be aware of these variations to avoid misinterpretations. For example, eye contact, physical proximity, and handshakes may hold different meanings in different cultures. Educate yourself on cultural norms to ensure that your nonverbal cues align with the intended message.

4. Communication Etiquette:

Cultural norms dictate communication etiquette, including the appropriate level of formality, greetings, and expressions of respect. Familiarize yourself with the customs and etiquette of different cultures to navigate conversations respectfully. Use appropriate titles and honorifics, follow greeting rituals, and adapt your communication style to match the cultural expectations.

5. High-Context vs. Low-Context Communication:

Cultures can be categorized as high-context or low-context based on their communication styles. High-context cultures rely on shared context, unspoken assumptions, and indirect communication, while low-context cultures prioritize explicit communication and clarity. Understanding these differences can help you adapt your communication to effectively convey your message and comprehend others' intentions.

6. Listening and Feedback:

Cultural differences also influence listening and feedback patterns. Some cultures emphasize active listening and encourage feedback, while others prioritize silence and respect for authority. Be mindful of these variations and adapt your listening and feedback approaches accordingly. Respect diverse communication styles and create a safe space for individuals to express their thoughts and opinions.

7. Avoiding Stereotypes and Generalizations:

While cultural awareness is crucial, it's essential to avoid stereotyping or making generalizations about individuals based on their cultural background. Recognize that diversity exists within cultures, and individuals may have unique communication preferences and styles. Treat each person as an individual and engage in open, respectful dialogue to understand their unique perspective.

8. Empathy and Open-Mindedness:

Cultivate empathy and open-mindedness when engaging in cross-cultural communication. Seek to understand the cultural context, values, and beliefs that shape others' communication styles. Show respect for diverse perspectives and be open to learning from different cultural backgrounds. Embrace the opportunity to broaden your worldview through meaningful intercultural interactions.

9. Cultural Intelligence:

Develop cultural intelligence, which encompasses knowledge, awareness, and skills related to cultural differences. Educate yourself about various cultures, their communication norms, and historical backgrounds. Build your cultural intelligence by engaging in cross-cultural experiences, interacting with individuals from different cultures, and seeking feedback to improve your intercultural communication skills.

10. Continuous Learning and Growth:

Cultural awareness and effective cross-cultural communication are ongoing processes. Cultures evolve, and new cultural encounters arise. Embrace a growth mindset and commit to continuous learning. Stay curious, seek opportunities to engage with diverse cultures, and reflect on your own cultural biases and assumptions. Actively strive to improve your intercultural communication skills.

Conclusion:

Understanding cultural differences in communication is crucial for effective cross-cultural interactions. By cultivating cultural sensitivity, adapting your communication style, respecting nonverbal cues, and practicing empathy, you can bridge cultural gaps and foster meaningful connections. Embrace continuous learning and strive to become a culturally competent communicator to navigate the diverse and interconnected world we live in.

Subchapter 2: Cross-Cultural Communication Challenges and Solutions

Introduction:

Cross-cultural communication brings unique challenges due to differences in language, customs, and communication styles. In this subchapter, we will explore common challenges faced in cross-cultural communication and provide strategies to overcome them.

1. Language Barriers:

Language barriers can hinder effective communication. When encountering language differences, use simple and clear language, avoid slang and idioms, and speak slowly and clearly. Utilize translation tools or interpreters when necessary. Additionally, learning basic phrases and greetings in the language of the culture you are interacting with can demonstrate respect and facilitate communication.

2. Misinterpretation of Nonverbal Cues:

Nonverbal cues can vary across cultures, leading to misinterpretation. Be aware of the potential differences in body language, gestures, and facial expressions. When in doubt, ask for clarification or use verbal communication to ensure that the intended message is conveyed accurately. Cultivate cultural sensitivity and adapt to the nonverbal communication norms of the culture you are engaging with.

3. Different Communication Styles:

Different cultures have distinct communication styles, such as direct or indirect communication. Recognize and adapt to these styles to avoid misunderstandings. If you are unsure about the preferred communication style, observe and learn from local customs or seek guidance from individuals familiar with the culture. Flexibility and open-mindedness are key in navigating diverse communication styles.

4. Stereotypes and Assumptions:

Stereotypes and assumptions based on cultural backgrounds can hinder effective communication. Be conscious of your own biases and avoid making assumptions about individuals based on their culture. Treat each person as an individual and approach communication with curiosity and openness. Engage in active listening and seek to understand the unique perspectives of others.

5. Differences in Etiquette and Customs:

Etiquette and customs vary greatly among cultures. Research and familiarize yourself with the cultural norms and customs of the individuals or communities you are interacting with. Respect local customs regarding greetings, personal space, and other social norms. When in doubt, observe and follow the lead of locals, and be willing to adapt your behavior to show respect and avoid unintentional offense.

6. Time and Punctuality:

Perceptions of time and punctuality can differ across cultures. Some cultures prioritize strict adherence to schedules, while others have a more flexible approach. Be mindful of these differences and adjust your expectations accordingly. When working with individuals from different cultural backgrounds, set clear expectations and communicate deadlines explicitly to avoid confusion.

7. Cultural Context and Implicit Meaning:

Cultural context plays a significant role in communication, and meanings can be implicit and indirect. Take the time to understand the cultural context and subtext behind messages. Seek clarification when needed and avoid jumping to conclusions. Building relationships and trust can help establish a deeper understanding of cultural nuances over time.

8. Empathy and Cultural Sensitivity:

Empathy and cultural sensitivity are essential in cross-cultural communication. Put yourself in the shoes of others and strive to understand their cultural perspectives and values. Be patient and tolerant, acknowledging that different cultures have their own unique communication approaches. Cultivate an attitude of respect and appreciation for diverse cultural backgrounds.

9. Active Learning and Curiosity:

Approach cross-cultural communication with a mindset of active learning and curiosity. Seek opportunities to engage with different cultures, ask questions, and listen attentively to gain insights and broaden your perspective. Embrace the opportunity for personal growth and challenge preconceived notions through intercultural experiences.

10. Continuous Learning and Feedback:

Cross-cultural communication is a continuous learning journey. Seek feedback from individuals from different cultural backgrounds to improve your communication skills. Reflect on your experiences and make adjustments accordingly. Stay updated on cultural trends and changes to remain culturally competent in your interactions.

Conclusion:

Cross-cultural communication challenges can be overcome through awareness, adaptability, empathy, and continuous learning. By embracing cultural differences, being mindful of communication styles, and seeking to understand others' perspectives, you can foster effective cross-cultural communication and build strong connections across diverse cultural contexts.

Subchapter 3: Cultivating Cultural Sensitivity in Communication

Introduction:

Cultural sensitivity is vital in effective communication, as it promotes understanding, respect, and inclusivity across diverse cultural contexts. In this subchapter, we will explore strategies to cultivate cultural sensitivity in communication.

1. Self-Reflection and Awareness:

Begin by reflecting on your own cultural background, biases, and assumptions. Develop self-awareness regarding your beliefs, values, and communication patterns. Acknowledge and challenge any preconceived notions or stereotypes you may hold. This self-reflection lays the foundation for cultivating cultural sensitivity.

2. Education and Learning:

Invest time in learning about different cultures, their histories, customs, and communication norms. Read books, articles, and watch documentaries that provide insights into diverse cultural perspectives. Attend cultural events, workshops, or courses to deepen your understanding. Embrace the opportunity to expand your knowledge and challenge cultural stereotypes.

3. Open-Mindedness and Curiosity:

Approach cultural differences with an open mind and a genuine curiosity to learn. Avoid making assumptions or judgments based on cultural stereotypes. Instead, engage in active listening and ask questions to understand others' perspectives. Embrace the diversity of experiences and views that different cultures offer.

4. Respect for Cultural Differences:

Respect for cultural differences is crucial in fostering cultural sensitivity. Appreciate the uniqueness of each culture and demonstrate respect for their customs, traditions, and values. Avoid imposing your own cultural norms on others and instead embrace the opportunity to learn from different perspectives.

5. Adaptability and Flexibility:

Cultivate adaptability and flexibility in your communication style. Recognize that different cultures may have different preferences for directness, formality, or assertiveness. Adapt your communication approach to align with the cultural context you are engaging with. Be willing to modify your communication style while maintaining authenticity and respect.

6. Active Listening and Empathy:

Practice active listening and empathy when communicating with individuals from different cultures. Listen attentively, seek to understand their perspectives, and validate their experiences. Show empathy by acknowledging the influence of cultural backgrounds on their communication styles. This fosters trust, understanding, and meaningful connections.

7. Nonverbal Communication Awareness:

Develop an understanding of nonverbal cues specific to different cultures. Be aware of variations in body language, eye contact, and personal space. Respect cultural differences in greetings, gestures, and physical contact. Pay attention to nonverbal signals and adapt your own nonverbal communication to align with the cultural norms of the context.

8. Patience and Tolerance:

Cultivating cultural sensitivity requires patience and tolerance. Recognize that misunderstandings may occur due to cultural differences in communication. Be patient in navigating these challenges, seek clarification when needed, and approach conflicts with a willingness to understand and find common ground. Embrace the opportunity to learn from these experiences.

9. Building Relationships:

Building relationships across cultures is a powerful way to cultivate cultural sensitivity. Foster meaningful connections with individuals from diverse cultural backgrounds. Engage in open, respectful dialogue, and seek to understand their perspectives. Through relationships, you can gain insights into different cultural contexts and deepen your cultural sensitivity.

10. Continuous Growth and Reflection:

Cultivating cultural sensitivity is an ongoing process. Regularly reflect on your communication experiences and interactions with individuals from different cultures. Identify areas for growth and improvement. Seek feedback from others and embrace opportunities to enhance your cultural sensitivity in communication.

Conclusion:

Cultivating cultural sensitivity in communication requires self-reflection, education, openness, and respect. By embracing cultural differences, adapting communication styles, and actively seeking to understand others, you can foster an inclusive and culturally sensitive approach to communication. Embrace continuous growth and reflection to enhance your cultural sensitivity skills over time.

Chapter 8: Communication in the Digital Age

Subchapter 1: Written Communication in the Digital World

Introduction:

In the digital age, written communication has become an integral part of our daily lives. In this subchapter, we will explore the nuances and strategies of effective written communication in the digital realm.

1. Clarity and Conciseness:

In digital written communication, clarity and conciseness are crucial. Use clear and simple language to convey your message effectively. Avoid long and complex sentences that can lead to confusion. Break down information into easily digestible paragraphs and use bullet points or numbered lists to organize your ideas.

2. Tone and Politeness:

Pay attention to the tone of your written communication. In the absence of face-to-face interaction, written messages can be easily misinterpreted. Choose words carefully and ensure your tone is respectful and polite. Avoid using aggressive or confrontational language. Consider the cultural context and use appropriate language to show respect and professionalism.

3. Formatting and Structure:

Optimize the formatting and structure of your written communication. Use headings, subheadings, and paragraphs to make your content more visually appealing and easy to navigate. Utilize appropriate formatting tools such as bold, italics, and underline to emphasize important points. Incorporate white space to improve readability.

4. Grammar and Proofreading:

Maintain proper grammar and punctuation in your written communication. Use grammar and spell-check tools to minimize errors. Proofread your content carefully before sending it, as errors can impact the clarity and professionalism of your message. Consider enlisting the help of a colleague or utilizing proofreading services to ensure accuracy.

5. Context and Audience Awareness:

Be mindful of the context and audience when crafting written communication. Adapt your language and style to suit the specific audience you are addressing. Consider their knowledge level, cultural background, and expectations. Tailor your message accordingly to ensure it resonates with your intended audience.

6. Email Etiquette:

Email is a common form of written communication in the digital world. Follow email etiquette guidelines such as using a professional email address, including a clear and concise subject line, and addressing recipients appropriately. Use proper salutations and closing remarks. Keep emails concise and focused, and avoid forwarding unnecessary messages.

7. Tone and Voice in Social Media:

When engaging in social media platforms, be mindful of your tone and voice. Maintain a consistent and authentic voice that aligns with your personal or professional brand. Be aware of the potential for misinterpretation due to the brevity and informality of social media posts. Exercise caution and ensure your messages are respectful and appropriate.

8. Netiquette and Online Communication:

Netiquette refers to the etiquette of online communication. Respect others' opinions and avoid engaging in online conflicts or offensive behavior. Use appropriate language and avoid writing in all caps (which is perceived as shouting) or using excessive emojis or abbreviations. Be mindful of cultural differences and communicate with sensitivity and inclusivity.

9. Digital Collaboration and Documentation:

Written communication plays a crucial role in digital collaboration and documentation. Use collaborative tools and platforms to streamline communication and document sharing. Clearly communicate deadlines, responsibilities, and expectations in collaborative projects. Maintain a record of important discussions and decisions for future reference.

10. Privacy and Data Security:

Ensure privacy and data security in your written communication. Be cautious when sharing sensitive information and use secure channels for confidential communication. Familiarize yourself with data protection regulations and follow best practices to safeguard personal and sensitive information.

Conclusion:

Effective written communication in the digital age requires clarity, conciseness, and cultural sensitivity. By paying attention to tone, formatting, grammar, and context, you can ensure your messages are understood and convey professionalism. Embrace digital etiquette, adapt your communication style to different platforms, and prioritize privacy and data security. Mastering written communication in the digital world enhances your overall communication effectiveness in today's interconnected society.

Subchapter 2: Effective Virtual Communication Strategies

Introduction:

With the rise of remote work and virtual interactions, effective virtual communication has become essential. In this subchapter, we will explore strategies to enhance virtual communication and foster meaningful connections in the digital realm.

1. Establish Clear Communication Channels:

Identify and establish clear communication channels for virtual interactions. Utilize platforms such as email, instant messaging, video conferencing, and project management tools to facilitate communication. Clearly communicate the preferred channels to team members and ensure everyone is on the same page.

2. Use Video Conferencing for Face-to-Face Interaction:

When possible, opt for video conferencing instead of solely relying on audio or text-based communication. Video conferencing allows for facial expressions, body language, and visual cues that enhance understanding and connection. It helps replicate the experience of in-person communication and fosters engagement among participants.

3. Set Clear Expectations and Guidelines:

Establish clear expectations and guidelines for virtual communication. Define communication norms, response times, and availability for team members. Clarify preferred modes of communication for different types of messages or situations. Setting expectations helps ensure smooth and efficient communication within virtual teams.

4. Active Listening and Engagement:

Practice active listening during virtual interactions. Give your full attention to the speaker, avoid distractions, and maintain eye contact through the camera. Engage in the conversation by nodding, using appropriate gestures, and providing verbal feedback. Active listening promotes understanding and connection in virtual settings.

5. Clear and Concise Written Communication:

Written communication remains important in virtual settings. Ensure your written messages are clear, concise, and easy to understand. Use proper grammar, punctuation, and formatting. Break down complex information into organized sections or bullet points. Consider the receiver's perspective and avoid ambiguity.

6. Embrace Visual Aids and Multimedia:

Utilize visual aids and multimedia to enhance virtual communication. Use slides, charts, and diagrams to illustrate complex concepts during presentations. Share relevant documents, images, or videos to support discussions. Visual aids increase engagement and understanding among participants.

7. Foster Collaboration and Participation:

Encourage collaboration and participation in virtual settings. Utilize collaboration tools that allow real-time document editing, brainstorming, and idea sharing. Allocate time for team members to contribute their thoughts and ideas. Create a safe and inclusive environment that promotes active involvement and creativity.

8. Be Mindful of Time Zones and Availability:

When collaborating with individuals across different time zones, be mindful of scheduling and availability. Respect others' working hours and find suitable meeting times that accommodate everyone's time zones as much as possible. Clearly communicate meeting times and expectations in advance to avoid confusion.

9. Develop Virtual Relationship-Building Strategies:

Virtual communication can lack the personal connections established through face-to-face interactions. Develop strategies to build relationships in virtual settings. Encourage informal conversations before or after meetings, dedicate time for team-building activities, or create virtual social spaces for casual interactions. Building relationships enhances trust and collaboration.

10. Adapt to Technological Challenges:

Virtual communication may encounter technological challenges. Be prepared to adapt and find alternative solutions. Have backup communication options available, ensure stable internet connectivity, and familiarize yourself with the features and troubleshooting options of virtual communication tools. Patience and flexibility are key when addressing technological hurdles.

Conclusion:

Effective virtual communication requires clear channels, active engagement, and adaptability to overcome challenges. By utilizing video conferencing, setting clear expectations, practicing active listening, and embracing visual aids, you can foster effective virtual communication and build strong connections in the digital realm. Prioritize collaboration, relationship-building, and technological preparedness to ensure successful virtual interactions.

Subchapter 3: Managing Online Communication Etiquette

Introduction:

With the increasing reliance on online communication, it's essential to navigate virtual interactions with proper etiquette. In this subchapter, we will explore strategies for managing online communication etiquette to maintain professionalism and foster positive relationships.

1. Use Proper Language and Tone:

Choose your words carefully and use appropriate language in online communication. Maintain a professional tone and avoid using slang, offensive language, or excessive jargon. Be mindful of cultural and regional differences, ensuring your messages are inclusive and respectful to all recipients.

2. Respectful and Constructive Feedback:

When providing feedback online, be respectful and constructive. Frame your feedback in a positive manner, focusing on specific observations and offering suggestions for improvement. Avoid personal attacks or public criticism. Maintain professionalism and empathy, recognizing the impact of your words on the recipient.

3. Mindful and Timely Responses:

Respond to online communication in a timely manner. Avoid delayed responses that may give the impression of disinterest or lack of professionalism. However, balance responsiveness with the need for thoughtful and considered replies. Be mindful of the urgency of the message and prioritize accordingly.

4. Practice Netiquette:

Follow netiquette guidelines to ensure respectful online interactions. Be polite, considerate, and courteous in your communication. Use proper salutations and closing remarks. Avoid typing in all caps (seen as shouting) or using excessive exclamation marks. Respect others' opinions and engage in healthy discussions.

5. Avoid Overcommunication:

While it's important to maintain effective communication, avoid overcommunication that can lead to information overload and email fatigue. Be concise and clear in your messages, avoiding unnecessary repetition. Consolidate information and use appropriate channels for specific purposes to streamline communication.

6. Privacy and Confidentiality:

Respect privacy and confidentiality in online communication. Be cautious when sharing sensitive information, ensuring you are using secure channels and appropriate encryption methods. Obtain consent before sharing others' personal or confidential information. Safeguard data and adhere to relevant privacy regulations.

7. Professional Email Practices:

When using email for professional communication, follow best practices. Use a professional email address, avoid using email as a platform for personal discussions, and include a clear subject line to convey the purpose of the email. Keep emails concise, organized, and focused on the topic at hand.

8. Mindful Social Media Presence:

Be mindful of your social media presence and its impact on your personal and professional life. Think before posting and consider the potential consequences of your words or actions. Maintain a positive and professional image, avoiding offensive or inflammatory content. Respect the boundaries of others and be mindful of online discussions.

9. Managing Online Conflicts:

In the event of online conflicts or disagreements, approach them with a calm and respectful demeanor. Avoid engaging in heated arguments or personal attacks. Take a step back, assess the situation objectively, and address the issue privately and professionally. Seek resolution through open dialogue and empathy.

10. Continuous Learning and Adaptation:

Online communication is dynamic and constantly evolving. Stay updated with emerging trends, tools, and best practices. Continuously learn and adapt your communication etiquette to new platforms and technologies. Seek feedback from colleagues or mentors to improve your online communication skills over time.

Conclusion:

Managing online communication etiquette is crucial for maintaining professionalism and fostering positive relationships. By using proper language and tone, practicing constructive feedback, being mindful of responses, and following netiquette guidelines, you can navigate virtual interactions with respect and professionalism. Protect privacy, practice professional email practices, and manage online conflicts with empathy and professionalism. Continuous learning and adaptation will help you stay current and effective in your online communication endeavors.

Chapter 9: Emotional Intelligence and Communication

Subchapter 1: Recognizing and Managing Emotions in Communication

Introduction:

Emotional intelligence plays a vital role in effective communication. In this subchapter, we will explore the importance of recognizing and managing emotions in communication to foster understanding, empathy, and positive connections.

1. Understanding Emotional Intelligence:

Begin by understanding the concept of emotional intelligence. Emotional intelligence refers to the ability to recognize, understand, and manage emotions, both in oneself and in others. It involves perceiving emotions accurately, using emotions to guide thinking and decision-making, and effectively managing emotions in interpersonal interactions.

2. Self-Awareness of Emotions:

Develop self-awareness of your own emotions during communication. Recognize and acknowledge your feelings, as they can influence your communication style and outcomes. Understand how certain emotions may impact your responses and adjust your communication accordingly. Practice mindfulness to stay attuned to your emotional state during interactions.

3. Empathy and Perspective-Taking:

Cultivate empathy and the ability to take others' perspectives. Empathy involves understanding and sharing the emotions of others. In communication, empathetic listening and understanding the emotions behind someone's words can foster deeper connections and mutual understanding. Practice active listening, ask clarifying questions, and validate others' emotions.

4. Emotional Regulation:

Develop strategies to regulate your emotions during communication. This involves managing emotional reactions that may hinder effective communication. Take a moment to pause and reflect before responding impulsively. Practice deep breathing or visualization techniques to maintain composure and prevent emotional outbursts. Focus on finding constructive solutions rather than dwelling on negative emotions.

5. Nonverbal Cues and Emotional Expression:

Pay attention to nonverbal cues and emotional expressions during communication. Body language, facial expressions, and tone of voice can convey emotions that may not be explicitly stated. Be aware of your own nonverbal cues and how they may impact others' interpretations. Interpret others' nonverbal cues to gain a deeper understanding of their emotional state.

6. Clear and Respectful Communication:

Ensure your communication is clear, respectful, and sensitive to emotions. Choose words carefully to express yourself effectively while considering the emotional impact on the recipient. Be mindful of the tone and delivery of your message, aiming for a balance between assertiveness and empathy. Use "I" statements to express your feelings and opinions without blaming or attacking others.

7. Conflict Resolution and Emotional Understanding:

In conflicts or difficult conversations, strive for emotional understanding and resolution. Recognize that emotions often underlie conflicts, and addressing these emotions can lead to more productive outcomes. Practice active listening, validate others' emotions, and find common ground to work towards a mutually satisfactory resolution.

8. Emotional Intelligence in Leadership:

Leaders can enhance their effectiveness by applying emotional intelligence in communication. Understand and respond to the emotions of team members, fostering a supportive and inclusive environment. Encourage open and honest communication while providing constructive feedback with empathy. Lead by example in managing emotions and promoting emotional intelligence within the team.

9. Continuous Development of Emotional Intelligence:

Emotional intelligence is a skill that can be developed over time. Seek opportunities for self-reflection and self-improvement. Take part in emotional intelligence workshops or training programs. Reflect on past interactions to identify areas for growth and practice applying emotional intelligence in various communication scenarios.

10. Practicing Mindful Communication:

Mindful communication involves being fully present and attentive in your interactions. Focus on the present moment, listen actively, and respond with intention. By practicing mindful communication, you can enhance your emotional intelligence, deepen connections, and foster meaningful relationships.

Conclusion:

Recognizing and managing emotions in communication is a key aspect of emotional intelligence. By developing self-awareness, practicing empathy, regulating emotions, and fostering clear and respectful communication, you can enhance your ability to connect with others and navigate interpersonal interactions effectively. Apply emotional intelligence in conflict resolution, leadership, and continuous self-development to foster positive and fulfilling communication experiences.

Subchapter 2: Empathy and Compassion in Communication

Introduction:

Empathy and compassion are essential elements of effective communication. In this subchapter, we will explore how empathy and compassion can enhance communication and contribute to building strong relationships.

1. Understanding Empathy:

Empathy involves understanding and sharing the emotions and experiences of others. It allows us to connect with others on a deeper level and respond to their needs with sensitivity. In communication, empathy helps create a safe and supportive environment where individuals feel heard and understood.

2. Practicing Active Listening:

Active listening is a fundamental aspect of empathy in communication. It involves giving your full attention to the speaker, seeking to understand their perspective, and responding with empathy. Maintain eye contact, use nonverbal cues to show engagement, and avoid interrupting. Reflect back on what the speaker is saying to demonstrate understanding.

3. Cultivating Emotional Awareness:

Develop emotional awareness to better understand the emotions of others. Pay attention to verbal and nonverbal cues, such as tone of voice, facial expressions, and body language. Notice subtle changes in emotions during conversations and adapt your communication style accordingly. Sensitivity to others' emotions allows for more empathetic responses.

4. Perspective-Taking:

Practice perspective-taking to enhance empathy in communication. Put yourself in the other person's shoes and try to understand their thoughts, feelings, and experiences. This helps you see the situation from their perspective and respond in a way that acknowledges their emotions and needs.

5. Validating Emotions:

Validation is a powerful tool in empathetic communication. Acknowledge and validate the emotions of others, even if you don't agree with their perspective. Let them know that their feelings are valid and understandable. Avoid dismissing or minimizing their emotions, as this can hinder effective communication and trust-building.

6. Expressing Empathy Verbally:

Verbalize your empathy to the person you are communicating with. Use phrases like "I understand how you feel" or "That must be challenging for you." Expressing empathy verbally shows that you are present and attentive to their emotions. It reassures them that their feelings are heard and acknowledged.

7. Responding with Compassion:

Compassion goes beyond empathy by incorporating a genuine concern for the well-being of others. In communication, compassion involves responding with kindness, understanding, and a desire to alleviate suffering. Show empathy through your words and actions, and offer support and assistance when appropriate.

8. Avoiding Judgment and Assumptions:

To maintain empathy and compassion in communication, avoid making judgments or assumptions about others. Each person has a unique perspective and experiences that shape their emotions. Be open-minded and suspend judgment to create an environment where individuals feel safe sharing their thoughts and feelings.

9. Nonverbal Communication of Empathy:

Nonverbal cues play a crucial role in conveying empathy and compassion. Maintain an open and welcoming posture, use facial expressions that reflect understanding and empathy, and provide comforting gestures when appropriate. Nonverbal communication can enhance the sincerity and impact of your empathetic responses.

10. Self-Reflection and Continuous Growth:

Regularly engage in self-reflection to assess your empathetic communication skills. Consider how your words and actions impact others and identify areas for improvement. Seek feedback from trusted individuals to gain insights into how your empathy is perceived. Engage in continuous growth by seeking learning opportunities and practicing empathy in various communication contexts.

Conclusion:

Empathy and compassion are powerful tools in effective communication. By practicing active listening, cultivating emotional awareness, and expressing empathy verbally, you can create a supportive and understanding communication environment. Responding with compassion and avoiding judgment, along with nonverbal cues of empathy, further enhance the connection with others. Engage in self-reflection and continuous growth to strengthen your empathetic communication skills and foster positive and meaningful relationships.

Subchapter 3: Using Emotional Intelligence to Build Trust and Understanding

Introduction:

Emotional intelligence plays a significant role in building trust and understanding in communication. In this subchapter, we will explore how emotional intelligence can be utilized to foster trust, enhance understanding, and strengthen relationships.

1. Developing Self-Awareness:

Self-awareness is the foundation of emotional intelligence. By understanding your own emotions, triggers, and communication style, you can better navigate interactions with others. Reflect on your strengths, weaknesses, and biases, and be conscious of how they may influence your communication and perceptions.

2. Active Listening and Empathy:

Active listening and empathy are crucial components of building trust and understanding. Practice active listening by giving your full attention, maintaining eye contact, and demonstrating genuine interest in the speaker's perspective. Empathize with others by seeking to understand their emotions and experiences, and validate their feelings.

3. Emotional Regulation:

Effective emotional regulation is key to building trust and understanding. Emotions can impact communication, and being able to regulate them in challenging situations is essential. Recognize and manage your emotions, staying calm and composed, even in difficult conversations. This allows for more thoughtful responses and avoids reacting impulsively.

4. Transparency and Authenticity:

Building trust requires transparency and authenticity in your communication. Be open and honest in expressing your thoughts and feelings, and avoid hidden agendas or manipulative tactics. Authenticity fosters genuine connections and helps others feel comfortable reciprocating trust and understanding.

5. Building Rapport:

Rapport-building is a critical aspect of fostering trust and understanding. Establish a positive connection with others by finding common ground, showing genuine interest, and practicing empathy. Use appropriate humor, engage in small talk, and demonstrate respect for diverse perspectives. Building rapport creates a foundation of trust and openness in communication.

6. Conflict Resolution with Emotional Intelligence:

Conflict is a natural part of relationships, and resolving conflicts requires emotional intelligence. Approach conflicts with empathy, seeking to understand all perspectives involved. Focus on finding mutually beneficial solutions rather than trying to "win" the argument. Use effective communication techniques, such as active listening and respectful dialogue, to reach resolutions that honor everyone's needs.

7. Cultivating Emotional Safety:

Create an emotionally safe environment where individuals feel comfortable expressing themselves openly. Avoid judgment, criticism, or ridicule. Encourage open dialogue and actively listen without interrupting. Respond with empathy and understanding, allowing for vulnerability and authentic communication.

8. Recognizing Nonverbal Cues:

Nonverbal cues can provide valuable insights into a person's emotions and intentions. Pay attention to body language, facial expressions, and tone of voice. Recognize when there may be incongruence between verbal and nonverbal cues, as this can indicate hidden emotions or underlying concerns. Respond sensitively to these cues to foster understanding.

9. Mindful Communication:

Mindful communication involves being present in the moment and fully engaged in the interaction. Avoid distractions and multitasking during conversations. Be attentive to the emotional needs of the speaker and respond with care. Mindful communication deepens understanding, fosters trust, and allows for more meaningful connections.

10. Continuous Learning and Improvement:

Emotional intelligence is a skill that can be developed and improved over time. Commit to continuous learning and self-improvement by seeking feedback from others, reflecting on your communication experiences, and seeking resources or training to enhance your emotional intelligence. Embrace opportunities for growth and apply your learnings in future interactions.

Conclusion:

Using emotional intelligence to build trust and understanding is essential for effective communication. By developing self-awareness, practicing active listening and empathy, regulating emotions, and fostering transparency and authenticity, you can create an environment of trust and understanding. Building rapport, resolving conflicts with empathy, and cultivating emotional safety further contribute to meaningful connections. Pay attention to nonverbal cues, practice mindful communication, and commit to continuous learning and improvement to strengthen your emotional intelligence skills and build lasting trust and understanding in your relationships.

Chapter 10: Communication in Leadership

Subchapter 1: Communication Skills for Effective Leadership

Introduction:

Effective leadership is closely tied to excellent communication skills. In this subchapter, we will explore the essential communication skills that leaders need to inspire, motivate, and guide their teams towards success.

1. Clear and Concise Communication:

Leaders must communicate their vision, goals, and expectations clearly and concisely. Avoid ambiguity and use simple language that everyone can understand. Break down complex information into digestible segments, ensuring that your message is easy to comprehend and remember.

2. Active Listening:

Active listening is a critical skill for leaders. Practice active listening by giving your full attention to the speaker, maintaining eye contact, and providing verbal and nonverbal cues that indicate engagement. Show genuine interest in others' perspectives, ideas, and concerns. This fosters trust, encourages open dialogue, and promotes a culture of collaboration.

3. Effective Feedback:

Providing constructive feedback is essential for leadership communication. Deliver feedback in a timely and specific manner, focusing on behaviors and results rather than personal attributes. Balance praise and recognition with areas for improvement, offering actionable suggestions for growth. Encourage a growth mindset and foster a supportive environment for continuous development.

4. Emotional Intelligence:

Leaders must demonstrate emotional intelligence in their communication. Understand and manage your emotions and be attuned to the emotions of others. Show empathy, validate feelings, and adapt your communication style to suit different individuals and situations. Emotional intelligence enables you to build strong relationships, inspire trust, and navigate challenges effectively.

5. Clarity of Purpose and Vision:

Leaders must effectively communicate their purpose and vision to inspire and align their teams. Clearly articulate the mission, values, and long-term goals of the organization. Connect the work of individuals to the larger purpose, helping them understand how their contributions contribute to the overall success. Regularly reinforce the vision to maintain focus and motivation.

6. Nonverbal Communication and Presence:

Leaders' nonverbal communication and presence play a significant role in influencing others. Pay attention to your body language, posture, facial expressions, and tone of voice. Project confidence, approachability, and enthusiasm. Use gestures and expressions to emphasize key points and demonstrate engagement. Your nonverbal cues should align with your verbal messages to reinforce authenticity and trust.

7. Storytelling and Inspirational Communication:

Effective leaders are skilled storytellers who can inspire and motivate others. Use storytelling techniques to convey your message, connect emotionally with your audience, and create a memorable impact. Craft narratives that highlight successes, challenges overcome, and the shared journey towards the vision. Inspire through your words, evoking passion, and igniting a sense of purpose.

8. Adaptability and Flexibility:

Leaders must be adaptable and flexible in their communication approach. Different situations and individuals may require varying communication styles. Recognize and adapt to the needs and preferences of your team members. Tailor your communication to resonate with different personalities, cultures, and communication channels. This adaptability strengthens relationships and promotes effective collaboration.

9. Effective Conflict Resolution:

Leaders must handle conflicts and disagreements with finesse and fairness. Facilitate open dialogue, ensuring all perspectives are heard. Practice active listening, mediate discussions, and seek win-win solutions. Encourage a culture of respectful and constructive conflict resolution, where differences are seen as opportunities for growth and innovation.

10. Transparency and Authenticity:

Leaders should strive for transparency and authenticity in their communication. Be honest and open with your team, sharing relevant information, successes, and challenges. Admit mistakes and take responsibility when necessary. Trust is built when leaders demonstrate authenticity and align their words with their actions.

Conclusion:

Communication skills are vital for effective leadership. By mastering clear and concise communication, practicing active listening, demonstrating emotional intelligence, and effectively conveying purpose and vision, leaders can inspire and motivate their teams. Nonverbal communication, storytelling, adaptability, and conflict resolution further enhance leadership communication. Embrace transparency and authenticity to build trust and foster a culture of open communication. Develop and refine these communication skills to become an impactful and influential leader.

Subchapter 2: Influential Communication in Management and Decision-making

Introduction:

Influential communication is crucial for effective management and decision-making. In this subchapter, we will explore the communication skills and strategies that managers can employ to influence others, facilitate decision-making processes, and drive positive outcomes.

1. Building Relationships and Trust:

Establishing strong relationships based on trust is essential for influential communication. Invest time in getting to know your team members, colleagues, and stakeholders. Foster an environment of mutual respect and open communication. Build trust by consistently demonstrating integrity, reliability, and transparency in your interactions.

2. Active Listening and Understanding:

Practice active listening to understand the perspectives and concerns of others. Give your full attention, maintain eye contact, and provide verbal and nonverbal cues that show engagement. Seek to understand different viewpoints and ask clarifying questions. This fosters trust, builds rapport, and helps you make informed decisions.

3. Effective Persuasion:

Develop effective persuasion skills to influence others' opinions and gain their support. Clearly articulate your ideas, presenting compelling arguments and evidence. Use logical reasoning and emotional appeals to connect with your audience. Tailor your communication style to resonate with different individuals and address their specific concerns or interests.

4. Communication Clarity and Simplicity:

Ensure your communication is clear, concise, and easy to understand. Avoid jargon or technical language that may confuse others. Use simple and straightforward language to convey your message effectively. Break down complex ideas into digestible pieces, using examples or visuals to enhance comprehension.

5. Data-driven Communication:

In management and decision-making, data plays a significant role. Use data to support your arguments, provide evidence, and justify your decisions. Present data in a visually appealing and understandable manner. Explain the relevance and implications of the data, helping others see the value in your proposals.

6. Negotiation and Compromise:

Effective negotiation skills are essential for influential communication in decision-making. Identify common ground, explore win-win solutions, and be open to compromise. Maintain a respectful and collaborative approach, seeking mutually beneficial outcomes. Active listening, empathy, and creative problem-solving are key elements of successful negotiations.

7. Emotional Intelligence in Decision-making:

Emotional intelligence is valuable in making informed decisions and effectively communicating them. Recognize and manage your own emotions, as well as those of others involved. Consider the emotional impact of decisions and communicate them sensitively. Show empathy and understanding, especially in challenging or sensitive situations.

8. Transparency and Inclusion:

Promote transparency and inclusion in decision-making processes. Involve relevant stakeholders and solicit their input and feedback. Communicate the rationale behind decisions, explaining how they align with organizational goals or priorities. Create opportunities for dialogue and address concerns or questions openly. Transparency and inclusion build trust and encourage ownership of decisions.

9. Confidence and Assertiveness:

Communicate with confidence and assertiveness to inspire trust and convey credibility. Express your ideas and opinions clearly, while respecting the perspectives of others. Use confident body language, maintain eye contact, and speak with conviction. Strike a balance between being assertive and receptive to different viewpoints.

10. Continuous Improvement and Feedback:

Embrace a culture of continuous improvement and seek feedback on your communication and decision-making skills. Reflect on past experiences, identify areas for growth, and actively work on refining your approach. Encourage feedback from others and be open to constructive criticism. By continuously developing your communication skills, you can enhance your influence and effectiveness as a manager.

Conclusion:

Influential communication is vital for effective management and decision-making. By building relationships based on trust, practicing active listening, developing persuasive skills, and promoting transparency and inclusion, managers can positively influence others. Utilize data-driven communication, emotional intelligence, and effective negotiation to make informed decisions. Cultivate confidence, continuous improvement, and feedback to refine your communication skills and become an influential manager.

Subchapter 3: Inspiring and Motivating through Communication

Introduction:

Effective leaders inspire and motivate their teams through powerful communication. In this subchapter, we will explore strategies and techniques for inspiring and motivating others through effective communication.

1. Articulating a Compelling Vision:

To inspire and motivate, leaders must articulate a compelling vision that aligns with the aspirations of their team members. Clearly communicate the purpose, goals, and values that guide your organization or project. Paint a vivid picture of the desired future, inspiring others to strive for excellence and invest their energy in achieving shared objectives.

2. Authenticity and Passion:

Authenticity is key to inspiring and motivating others. Show genuine passion and enthusiasm for your work and vision. Let your excitement and dedication shine through your words and actions. People are inspired by leaders who are authentic and genuinely invested in their mission.

3. Storytelling for Inspiration:

Harness the power of storytelling to inspire and connect with your team. Share stories that illustrate the impact of your work, highlighting successes, challenges overcome, and lessons learned. Craft narratives that evoke emotions and engage the imagination. Stories have the ability to inspire, instill a sense of purpose, and create a shared identity within the team.

4. Celebrating Successes and Recognizing Contributions:

Motivation thrives when successes are celebrated and individual contributions are recognized. Acknowledge and appreciate the achievements of your team members publicly. Highlight their specific contributions and the positive impact they have made. This not only motivates the individuals involved but also inspires others to strive for similar recognition.

5. Effective Communication Channels:

Choose communication channels that resonate with your team members and foster engagement. Consider different preferences for communication, such as team meetings, one-on-one discussions, emails, or digital collaboration platforms. Tailor your communication style to accommodate diverse needs, ensuring that your messages are received and understood by all.

6. Empowering and Delegating:

Inspire and motivate by empowering your team members and delegating meaningful responsibilities. Provide them with opportunities to take ownership of projects, make decisions, and showcase their skills. Communicate your trust in their abilities and offer support when needed. Empowered individuals feel motivated and valued, leading to increased productivity and job satisfaction.

7. Regular Communication and Feedback:

Maintain regular and open communication with your team members. Provide constructive feedback and guidance to help them grow and develop. Create a safe space for open dialogue, allowing team members to share their ideas, concerns, and aspirations. Be approachable and responsive, demonstrating that their voices are heard and valued.

8. Setting Challenging Goals:

Inspire and motivate by setting challenging but attainable goals for your team. Clearly communicate these goals and the rationale behind them. Encourage your team to stretch their capabilities and embrace new challenges. Provide support and resources to help them succeed. Well-defined goals inspire a sense of purpose and achievement.

9. Continuous Learning and Development:

Encourage a culture of continuous learning and development within your team. Communicate the importance of personal and professional growth. Provide opportunities for training, workshops, and mentorship. Inspire individuals to take ownership of their learning journey, fostering a sense of ambition and motivation.

10. Lead by Example:

As a leader, your actions speak louder than words. Lead by example and embody the values and behaviors you expect from your team. Demonstrate dedication, resilience, integrity, and a positive attitude. Your actions will inspire and motivate others to follow suit.

Conclusion:

Inspiring and motivating through communication requires a combination of vision, authenticity, storytelling, recognition, empowerment, and effective feedback. By articulating a compelling vision, being authentic and passionate, leveraging storytelling, celebrating successes, and empowering team members, you can create a motivating work environment. Foster regular communication, set challenging goals, encourage continuous learning, and lead by example to inspire and motivate your team to achieve their best.

Conclusion

Conclusion:

"Crafting Connections: The Art of Speech and the Power of Communication" has explored the various aspects of effective communication, providing insights and strategies to enhance our ability to connect with others, express ourselves clearly, and influence positive outcomes. Throughout the book, we have delved into the importance of communication, the elements of effective communication, and overcoming barriers that hinder effective exchange of ideas.

We started by understanding the significance of communication in our personal and professional lives, recognizing its power to build relationships, foster understanding, and drive success. We explored the elements of effective communication, including active listening, empathy, and the power of words, as well as honing our skills in public speaking and storytelling. We recognized the role of nonverbal communication, cultural awareness, and adapting to different communication styles in connecting with diverse audiences.

The book also emphasized the role of communication in leadership, interpersonal relationships, and the digital age. We discovered the importance of emotional intelligence, transparency, and adaptability in effective communication. We explored strategies for nurturing professional relationships, networking, and managing online communication etiquette.

Furthermore, the book highlighted the significance of influential communication in management, decision-making, and inspiring others. We explored the skills needed to motivate and inspire through communication, such as articulating a compelling vision, being authentic, using storytelling, recognizing contributions, empowering team members, and setting challenging goals.

In conclusion, "Crafting Connections: The Art of Speech and the Power of Communication" has provided a comprehensive guide to mastering the art of communication. By embracing the principles and techniques discussed in this book, readers can enhance their communication skills, build stronger relationships, and effectively navigate personal and professional challenges. Communication is the key to understanding, collaboration, and positive change, and by crafting connections through effective communication, we can create a world where ideas are shared, understood, and valued.

www.ingramcontent.com/pod-product-compliance
Lightning Source LLC
Chambersburg PA
CBHW060845220526
45466CB00003B/1247